Perfectly Normal

Perfectly Normal

A Mother's Memoir

Marcy Sheiner

People with Disabilities Press,
Stanley D. Klein, Ph.D., Series Editor
iUniverse, Inc.
San Jose New York Lincoln Shanghai

Perfectly Normal
A Mother's Memoir

People with Disabilities Press,
Stanley D. Klein, Ph.D., Series Editor
iUniverse, Inc.
an imprint of iUniverse, Inc.

For information address:
iUniverse, Inc.
5220 S. 16th St., Suite 200
Lincoln, NE 68512
www.iuniverse.com

ISBN: 0-595-21544-0

Printed in the United States of America

For Daryl, who taught me so much

I would not leave you in times of trouble.
We never could have come this far.
I took the good times. I'll take the bad times.
I'll take you just the way you are.

—*Billy Joel*

Contents

ACKNOWLEDGMENTS

I worked on this book for over twenty-five years, during which I periodically put it away, sometimes for a few months, sometimes for a few years, because at various points I became hopelessly stuck. I got stuck in rage; I got stuck in terror—but most of all I got stuck in the writer's hell of self-censorship. I knew that if I told the truth about what motherhood has been like for me, I would be breaking an ancient taboo, violating a conspiracy of silence that serves nothing less than keeping the human race going. Further, if I wrote about how difficult motherhood has been for me, I would open myself to the irrational charge, frequently leveled against mothers who complain, grumble, or in any way deviate from the norm, that I don't sufficiently love my children. If I told the truth about how painful motherhood has been for me, I would be seen as defective, unnatural, inhuman. Worst of all, if my children were to read what I wrote, I would, even at this late date, do them irreparable harm. I would be vulnerable to the most deadly epithet known to woman: "A Bad Mother."

I'm no stranger to artistic criticism: having written and published a great deal in the field of sex writing, I've received my share of social censure. My work has been condemned, if not specifically, then certainly in its collective genre. Because of the heavy criticism heaped upon those who write honestly about sex, many people who do so consider themselves to be daring pioneers. While I agree that it's not easy to come out publicly in favor of sexual freedom, my work in that genre has never made me feel particularly daring. That's because the scariest place that I've ever ventured with my pen has been into the territory of motherhood.

That said, I would like to acknowledge all those who encouraged me to write and publish this story—Cara Bruce, Phyllis Christopher, James Green, Sandra Marilyn, Susan Miller, Shar Rednour, and Jackie Strano. If there's anyone I've forgotten, please forgive me.

For a lifetime of friendship, love and creative inspiration I am more than grateful to Angie D'Aries. Kathy Castellano, also remains an important person in my life, no matter how little we actually see each other. Darlene McGuire was a catalyst for my growth as a parent, and has, without even trying, changed the lives of everyone who knows her.

I would like to thank the Hydrocephalus Association and its founder/director, Emily Fudge, for their excellent work educating the public and advocating for people with hydrocephalus and their families. I also owe a debt of gratitude to those on the front lines of the Disability Rights Movement; they are too numerous to name, but in particular I'd like to thank Cheryl Marie Wade and Nancy Ferreyra. The fascinating and brilliant people in this community have taught me more than I could have possibly learned on my own, and they make this planet a kinder and safer place to live.

Thanks to Stan Klein who provided me with a forum to finally publish this book.

The two most important people in my life are the people who lived and breathed this story: my daughter Stacy, and my son Daryl. They're the reason that I continue to believe that life, no matter how difficult, is ultimately worth the struggle.

"If we who are raising children now speak the truth, finally we will be able to see."
— Susan Griffin

In 1956 my brand new transistor radio brought me the startling news of a pair of twins born with their heads stuck together. My ten-year-old imagination took flight, boggled by the possibilities. Did they share a brain? How would they walk? Most of all, what did they actually look like?

Excited, I ran home to deliver the news to my mother and my aunt, who was pregnant at the time. "Maybe," I said hopefully, "you'll have babies with their heads stuck together." My aunt gasped. My mother slapped me across the face.

Wounded, I shut myself into my room to reflect on what I'd done wrong, but try as I might, I could come up with no rational explanation for my mother's and aunt's behavior. Apparently, these marvelous creatures I'd heard about weren't considered so marvelous by the grown-ups. It would be many years before I understood why.

1

A Child Is Born

August 3, 1965.

I awoke to find myself in a room with a woman sitting up in the bed next to mine, pulling metal rollers out of her long brown hair.

"Hi," she said cheerily. "My name's Jackie. God, am I glad for some company. Now that I'm leaving tomorrow they finally bring someone in here. Isn't it always the way?"

I smiled uncertainly through a sodium pentathol induced haze.

"I had a boy too," Jackie continued. "They'll be coming around for feeding soon. You'd better let the nurse know you're up if you want to see yours."

Without hesitation I obeyed this stranger who, by virtue of having given birth a day or two before me, qualified as an authority.

The nurse appeared in less than a minute, whirling through the room flinging open curtains, flicking imaginary specks off the sink. "Oh, so you're up, Mama," she said with a nod in my direction. "Have you urinated or had a bowel movement yet?"

I shook my head, remembering my sister Linda's vivid descriptions of the excretion ceremonies on the maternity ward; I knew if I didn't urinate they'd catherize me, an altogether unpleasant affair, and that I wouldn't be allowed to leave the hospital until I'd emptied my bowels.

I strained on the bedpan, examining my body. My belly was loose and flabby, still patterned by purple stretch marks: so, I was stuck with them for life. My vagina was a pathetic mess, having been not only assaulted by a razor, but cut and stitched as well, episiotomies being as much a routine of childbirth as cutting the umbilical cord.

1

"Have you done it yet?" called the nurse.

"Not yet."

"Well, dear, I'm going to have to catherize you."

Threatened with invasion, my bladder immediately released a healthy stream of urine. When the nurse returned with her equipment, she actually seemed disappointed.

"And now are you mommies ready for your babies?" Jackie and I nodded eagerly.

My newborn son slept in a tiny glass box perched atop four wheeled legs. At first sight he resembled my grandfather, or any old man, his red face scrunched up in denial of his new surroundings. The nurse gave him to me with a bottle of water. He took a few weak sucks, then fell back asleep. Jackie's baby sucked avidly.

"Don't worry," she assured me. "Mine didn't drink the first day either."

Holding Daryl, I felt far older than my 19 years. For the first time I questioned my decision not to breast-feed—I had thought it old-fashioned, an activity suitable only for cows, an attitude enthusiastically endorsed by my family, friends, and doctor. Well, it was too late now—I'd been given pills to dry up my milk.

Surreptitiously I unfolded the blanket and took a quick inventory: ten toes, ten fingers, all in the right places. One tiny limp penis. Relieved, I closed my eyes and leaned against the pillow.

Jackie's voice startled me. "Aren't you glad he's all right? I was terrified something would be wrong with my baby. But thank God, he's perfectly normal."

"Yes," I breathed, recalling the nightmares: attacks on my swollen stomach, hideous creatures clinging to my vaginal walls.

Every pregnant woman harbors the fear that something will be 'wrong' with her baby—but to give voice to such thoughts during the nine months of gestation would be to give them greater credence; admitting those fears is as much a part of the afterbirth as the bloody placenta.

In the evening visitors filled our room. Jackie's husband and mother stood quietly by her bed, while my mother, father, sister and Bob, my husband, filled the rest of the space.

"Hey toots," my father boomed affectionately, giving me a wet kiss, grinning from ear to ear. When he smiled, his cheeks reddened like tiny apples in his shiny round face.

My mother pecked the air near my cheek, then took up a position at the foot of the bed. She stared without self-consciousness at Jackie's family and asked in a loud voice, "What did she have?"

"A boy too," I murmured, wishing that for once my mother would keep her voice down. But she went on, talking about the nurses, the hospital décor, her disdain of the crosses on the walls.

"It's a Catholic hospital, Ma," I said in a low warning voice.

"Yes I know," she replied, her words dripping with animosity. The only aspect of Judaism practiced in my family, so far as I'd ever been able to make out, was an active dislike of *the goyim*.

Bob had brought a bouquet of roses, and Linda ran off in search of a vase. When she returned she made a great fuss with them, searching for a knife to cut the stems, filling the vase, arranging them just so. This domesticity was totally out of character; I wanted my older sister to sit down and commiserate with me about the maternity ward, but she seemed to be avoiding any intimacy.

Bob's face was covered with thick stubble, rendering his dark olive skin even darker. He slouched in the corner chair next to my bed, inexplicably subdued.

My father grinned from ear to ear, and my mother sported her usual stiff smile, worn through thick and thin—but I had the uneasy sense that they were disappointed in me. Maybe it was because I'd had a boy—in my family we coveted female babies, dolls to dress up and show off.

Everything was discordant. Feeling acutely uncomfortable, I felt a sudden unstoppable urge to pee—a tedious event that involved pouring a pitcher of water over my stitched bottom in lieu of toilet paper, a procedure which everyone in the room could not avoid hearing. I should have been embarrassed, but I was too caught up in more confusing emotions, and the bathroom afforded me an escape from the claustrophobic atmosphere.

The next morning my obstetrician, a young crew-cutted fellow with an upturned nose and pasty skin, came in to check on me. As he poked at my breasts, lumpy with the strain of unreleased milk, he mumbled, "We're a little concerned about the shape of the baby's head. We're going to run some tests to see if he has hydrocephalus."

Life stopped. My heart skipped a beat; my facial muscles froze. The world narrowed, and it would never, never look the same again.

"What are you talking about? What's hydrocephalus?"

"Oh," he said casually, "it's a disease that causes the head to grow abnormally." He pulled up the sheet and headed for the door; hesitating, he groped for a comforting phrase. "Don't worry," he finally managed, "you can have more kids."

I sat there, totally stunned. So that was why everyone had behaved so oddly the night before: something was wrong with my baby. I should have known, dammit—should have known that a girl as clumsy as my mother always said I was could never pull off an uncomplicated birth.

Jackie broke the cold silence. "You're worried about what he said, aren't you?"

"Yeah. What's he talking about?"

"Oh, I wouldn't worry, it didn't sound too serious." She hid her face behind a hand mirror, and didn't speak to me again. I hardly noticed when she packed up and left the hospital with her baby, but sat immobilized, thinking not of my baby's probable pain, not of the uncertain future, but of the past: the past nine months. What had I done wrong?

I had conceived under less than ideal conditions: in the backseat of a car, unmarried. In a panic, I married a man who was a virtual stranger to me.

During my pregnancy I'd had a vaginal infection, and, having no notion of what the itching signified, felt too ashamed to tell the doctor.

I had watched my weight rather than nutrition, starving myself prior to checkups, and was proud to gain only sixteen pounds total—dieting was encouraged by my doctor, who'd asserted that "eating for two is an old wives' tale"—but now this became another one of my personal wrongdoings.

In my ninth month I'd gone swimming in a public pool, only to learn later that some doctors advised against this.

Last, but certainly not least, I had made love beyond the allotted time limit, up until three short weeks ago.

The litany never ended. With each passing day, year, decade, new sins were added to the list. Cigarettes. Coffee. Alcohol. Aspirin. I devoured reports of new medical discoveries, acquiring ammunition against myself. Sodium pentathol: I should have had natural childbirth. Radiation in cow's milk: I should have been drinking soymilk. Zinc. Calcium. Iron pills. Every time that child cried in pain or staggered under the weight of his head, my heart would cry out *mea culpa*.

Foggily I climbed out of bed to join the other mothers walking up and down the corridors in their new E.J. Korvette bathrobes. I saw them as characters in a science fiction movie, machines that had fulfilled their baby-making function, now useless and bored. I don't know, maybe they were walking around in a state of grace, ecstasy even, but as I said, the world had narrowed.

Or perhaps it had widened.

◆   ◆   ◆

I walked to the pay telephone and began dialing Bob's office, but stopped midway, remembering his demeanor the previous night: surely he had known. He had known something was wrong with our baby and he'd deliberately kept it from me. I hung up the receiver and sat in the phone booth absorbing this information.

Never had I felt so betrayed. However well-intentioned were Bob's motives in withholding vital information from me, I would never fully recover from this sense of betrayal; if we'd been strangers when we'd married, we were now well on our way to becoming enemies.

I picked up the phone again and called my sister.

"Linda? I just found out that the baby might have something called hydrocephalus."

"Dammit. Who told you?"

Again the bottom fell out of my world. "You mean you knew?"

"Well, Bob didn't want you to know until you'd had a chance to recover from the birth, so we all had to act like nothing was wrong."

My husband. My sister. My parents. I was surrounded by a band of lying traitors.

Stunned, I walked slowly back to my room. Bob was sitting in the armchair next to the bed. He didn't notice me at first, so for a minute I was able to observe him. Suddenly he seemed smaller than his six-foot-four and two hundred pounds, weaker than the burly football player he was, more vulnerable than the barroom bouncer he'd been when I'd met him. My anger at him dissolved, as I realized that he too was suffering. This baby was his child also; his first child; his son—with all the weight that word carries for a man like Bob. He looked up and, seeing me, opened his big bear arms. I fell into them, sobbing.

Silently we comforted each other. Finally I said, "To tell you the truth I can't imagine this happening to anyone else we know."

"What do you mean—you think we're losers?" he asked.

"Yeah," I said softly, feeling a great wave of shame flood over me. "That's what I mean."

I had, after all, failed the greatest test of womanhood—for women ultimately prove their worth by bearing healthy children. Indeed, in the recovery room Bob had whispered, "You came through with flying colors, kid." Now I'd learned that I had not, in fact, delivered flawlessly.

I had not been a rockbed of self-esteem to begin with; now I felt as if some inner deformity had manifested itself in my child, who would henceforth provide living proof of my defectiveness.

The hospital suspended normal visitation rules, allowing Bob to stay with me all day. On and off I cried, on and off I raged. I wanted the baby to live. I wanted the baby to die. I wanted the baby not to have this disease with the evil-sounding name.

When Daryl was brought in for feeding again, I studied him with a more critical eye. I saw what I'd missed before: his head was only slightly larger than normal, but asymmetrical. Tentatively I touched it: it seemed so vulnerable, he was so vulnerable. I felt a fierce desire to protect him, and at the same time, a certain amount of fear—not fear of what might happen to him, but an inexplicable fear of *him*, of his strangeness.

My parents came to visit again; this time we had the room to ourselves. My mother stood at the foot of the bed, smiling brightly, chattering inanely.

"We're getting the room ready," she said. No preparations had been made before I went into labor, out of the traditional Jewish superstition that this might hex the outcome of the pregnancy. Thinking of this archaic ritual and how it so obviously meant nothing, I laughed bitterly and said, "Ma, you do know about the baby, don't you?"

"Know what?"

"About the hydrocephalus."

"Oh, that. So, he'll have an operation."

Her characteristic lack of emotion suddenly enraged me. "You don't care, do you?" I shouted. "You don't even care!"

Her smile never wavered, but her eyes burned like dry ice, imparting their usual message: *Get control of yourself.*

I had no intention of getting control of myself: my mother had known something was wrong with my baby, and had marched in here smiling. Worse, she had somehow led me to this hospital bed with never a hint at what might transpire. A husband might betray, a father, even a sister—but a mother was not supposed to betray.

"You're like some kind of robot," I shouted, sobbing hysterically. The nurse, who must've heard the commotion, came scurrying in.

"Visiting hours are over," she announced briskly, shooing everyone out, though there were at least another fifteen minutes left. After she'd emptied the room, she returned with my usual vitamin pill and, beside it, a new pink capsule.

"What's this?" I asked.

"Just a little something to help you sleep."

Dutifully I swallowed my "medicine" and awoke the next morning not only refreshed but optimistic. Suddenly I, like my mother, felt that nothing was terribly wrong. When I thought about it, what was the big deal, after all? My baby had a medical problem; the doctors would fix it; and we would all live happily ever after.

The pediatrician came to explain my baby's condition and probable operation. Hydrocephalus, he told me, is a disease of the central nervous system wherein cerebro-spinal fluid, rather than circulating normally, accumulates in the head, causing it to grow rapidly and exerting pressure on the brain. The word literally translates as "water on the brain," a phrase commonly used to denote stupidity in popular "jokes," a phrase that would from this day forward cause me to cringe reflexively. In the past, I learned, babies with hydrocephalus either outgrew the condition—sometimes with brain damage—or died. In the late 1950s an operation was devised wherein a plastic tube, or shunt, is inserted beneath the scalp, stretching into the chest or stomach cavity, draining the fluid. Daryl's head was only slightly larger than a normal infant's, so his prognosis was good.

Under the effect of pills, which I never suspected until years later were mood elevators, I began to view Daryl's condition as if it were no more significant than a mole or a wart.

When my obstetrician came in later, he asked if the pediatrician had been to see me.

"Oh sure," I said, waving my arm in the air. "He told me all about hydrocephalus. Did you know Winston Churchill had it and he outgrew it?"

"No, I didn't," said my doctor, frowning as he checked my breasts.

"Well, he did. But I guess Daryl's going to need an operation."

"Hm. Well, anyhow, you can have more kids."

I snapped my gum in his face, mentally willing him out of my consciousness. "Daryl is going to be fine," I said, despising him.

My grandfather called to suggest institutionalizing the baby.

"Just think," he reasoned, "you'll be stuck for the rest of your life."

"He's going to be fine, Grampa," I said. I rolled my eyes at Bob, who was trying to follow the conversation, and mouthed something about my senile old grandfather. "He just needs an operation."

A friend who'd heard something was "wrong" with my baby telephoned.

"Oh," I said casually in response to the concern in Louann's voice, "he has something called hydrocephalus. They're going to do an operation and then he'll be okay."

"Thank God," she said. I could almost hear the rosary beads clicking in her devout Catholic hands. "At least it isn't a missing limb or something really bad."

"Oh, no, nothing like that. Really. He'll be fine."

Bob was astounded by my change in attitude. Beneath my bravado and drug-induced oblivion, though, I was feeling more and more isolated from the mainstream of humanity, a feeling that would intensify and affect me for the rest of my life. There were those who, like my grandfather, acted as if Daryl's birth was a dire tragedy, while others, like Louann, were relieved that he didn't have "something really bad." Both attitudes denied reality. Neither left room for my complex bundle of feelings.

But deep in the stillness of the hospital night, I took out a pen and paper and wrote a long letter to Angie, who'd been my best and closest friend since we'd met as fourteen-year-old high school sophomores. Shortly after graduation she'd gone off to Japan to marry her Navy boyfriend, and was now herself pregnant.

Dear Angie, I began, *There cannot possibly be a God.*

Surely this would end our years of theosophical debate, during which she had almost persuaded me to convert to Catholicism. At seventeen, I finally rejected her religion as well as any belief in God, but we still debated the matter with great passion. Now at last she would see my point of view: she would have to admit that no God would inflict pain and injustice upon an innocent baby. Of course, I was really writing about the pain and injustice inflicted upon *me*. I told her, letting loose the flood of emotions I hadn't expressed to anyone else, just how heart-broken I was. When I'd finished the letter and read it over several times, I firmly sealed the envelope. There. I'd had my say. Would Angie at least hear me? If she, who understood me so well, didn't understand me now, then there was no hope that anyone on this earth ever would.

For who could ever understand the depth of my disappointment?

I may have gotten pregnant by default, but the truth was, I had wanted a baby for as long as I could remember. I adored my little cousins, and once I was respectably married, I'd been ecstatic to be pregnant— in fact, I'd admitted guiltily to Linda that I had, at least subconsciously, engineered my pregnancy. I basked in the doting smiles of strangers as my belly grew, and devoured books on child rearing. I fantasized dressing up my baby, taking her (invariably I imagined a her) out in the stroller, playing with dolls in our apartment. I couldn't wait to have my very own little baby, for in my limited experience, babies were delightful playthings.

Most parents eventually learn that babies are much more complicated than mere playthings. I learned it in one brutal day.

2

Baby Blues

August 6, 1965. The hospital discharged us with nothing more than a six-pack of Enfamil and the name of a local neurosurgeon. With friends and relatives offering names of specialists as well, we took Daryl home, to proceed on our own.

Back at our apartment I found Linda, my mother, and Bob's mother Sylvia in the bedroom, which they'd furnished with a crib, teddy bears and colored balloons. When I searched through my closet for something to wear, I was chagrined to find that, despite my limited weight gain, nothing I owned fit. I sat down on the bed and wept.

Linda, a rueful half-smile on her face, looked first at my mother, then at Sylvia; in a split second some secret knowledge passed among them before Linda proclaimed, "Well, this must be your day for the baby blues!"

I immediately stopped crying: the phrase "baby blues" seemed cause for celebration. Never mind the state of my body, never mind I had a sick baby on my hands: like every mother in history, I had a case of the infamous baby blues. It denoted passage from girlhood to womanhood. It meant, above all, that I was normal.

For the next few days, as I staggered through the mechanics of infant care, leaving a trail of broken bottles and spilled formula behind, I sought and found consolation in a newfound camaraderie with these older, wiser women. I would call one or another of them at all hours of the day or night, panicked by what I saw as my incompetence, and they would laugh affectionately and give me advice.

Daryl threw up regularly—not just little spit-ups, but violent spasms called "projectile vomiting," a result of the pressure on his brain. Dutifully I washed his tiny clothes and, guiltily ignoring Dr. Spock, held him whenever he cried.

Linda, who worked nearby, came over every day on her lunch hour. This welcome adult interaction had me happily preparing grilled cheese sandwiches or tuna salad, turf I felt more comfortable on than infant care. But Linda would frequently find me agitated; on one particularly difficult day, after Daryl had thrown up his cereal and two bottles of milk, I tossed him into the crib and left him howling while I scrubbed his cotton kimonos, tears streaming from my eyes.

"I can't stand this," I confessed out loud for the first time, as Linda rescued Daryl and held him on her shoulder. "I *hate* being a mother. Something must be wrong with me—I don't love him the way you're supposed to."

"*Supposed* to?" Linda put a now quiet Daryl down to nap. "Who says you're supposed to?"

"Everyone...you know...maternal instinct."

Linda let out a loud snort. "Maternal instinct is a crock of shit! I didn't love Derry the minute I laid eyes on her."

"You didn't?" I stopped crying.

"Nope." She stirred some Nescafé into a cup of hot water, lit an unfiltered cigarette, and flung her platinum mane back from her forehead. "Babies are people. You get to love them as you get to know them—just like any other people."

This was an entirely new concept, and I was vastly relieved to hear it. Still, I remained frightened of my baby and my feelings. My fear was not entirely uncommon among new mothers, and the reality check from my sister was helpful. But my situation was also unique, something not even she acknowledged.

Bob and I began the round of neurologists and neurosurgeons, driving into the city each day for medical consultations. The buildings changed but the scenario was always the same. We would sit side by side before some huge oak desk, Daryl on my lap, while a man in a white coat leaned back in his swivel chair, or bent earnestly toward us, as he explained hydrocephalus and its treatment. Sometimes he used diagrams of the skull and spinal cord to illustrate the flow of cerebro-spinal fluid through the body and the obstruction that caused Daryl's head to grow.

"I'd advise you not to wait too long," he'd say. "We can operate next week."

OR

"Why don't we wait a few weeks and see what happens—he might outgrow it, you know. Once we put a shunt in, he'll be dependent on it for the rest of his life."

Then the doctor would rise and emerge from behind his desk, pull a soft tape measure out of his pocket, and wrap it around Daryl's skull while I held him still. He'd make a note of the measurement, and then he'd push down on Daryl's fontanel with his fat fingers. I, who had been raised with strong admonitions against ever touching a baby's "soft spot" nearly fainted: they were obviously madmen.

Positively shell-shocked, I withdrew: during our visits I fed Daryl his bottle or quietly amused him, allowing the important business to be discussed between the men. At the end of each session Bob would turn to me in frank appeal.

"Is there anything you want to ask?" he'd say. Mutely I'd shake my head.

Just once, though, I did have a question: I asked where we might read about hydrocephalus.

"Don't read anything," said the doctor with a dismissing wave of his hand. "It'll only confuse you."

I did not open a medical encyclopedia to "H" for another six years.

Bob always asked about Daryl's prognosis.

"Well, we don't really know much about this—we've only been doing this operation for twelve years."

"How long do people with hydrocephalus generally live?"

"As I've said, we've only..."

"How old is your oldest patient?" Bob persisted.

"Let's see, I've got a darling girl, one of the first..."

He went on to tell us the girl's family history and her physical appearance, but did not reveal the vital information we sought.

Each consultation cost upwards of $50.00, but not for a moment did I think about the money. Fortunately, I didn't have to: since Bob was an insurance salesman, we'd gotten excellent coverage prior to Daryl's birth.

"This must be costing you a fortune!" Louann exclaimed when I told her about our search for a doctor.

"We have good insurance," I replied curtly, offended that she'd think money was even remotely on my list of worries.

I don't remember how we made the decision to have the local doctor perform the operation; we were confused by the various opinions we'd received, and there was simply no way of knowing for sure what would be the best course of action. With Daryl throwing up and crying half the night, time seemed to be running out. So at two weeks old he was admitted to our local hospital for tests and surgery.

Caring for Daryl up to now had been difficult. Visits to doctors had been frightening. But my first serious trauma as Daryl's mother came when they shaved my baby's head and injected a dye solution into his scalp for X-ray purposes. (The CAT, MRI and other diagnostic equipment had not yet been invented. I have since heard of one early case of hydrocephalus where the doctor made his diagnosis by shining a flashlight on the baby's head in a darkened bathroom.)

During the hours before surgery, Daryl, like any pre-operative patient, wasn't permitted to eat. I walked him up and down the hospital room while he cried uncomprehendingly and his tiny frame clutched against me in hunger spasms.

Feebly I patted his back, thinking, this is what an Indian woman, or a welfare mother, or any poor woman feels when there is no food for her child: helpless, powerless to nourish her baby.

"Do you want me to hold him?" Bob asked.

I shook my head and continued to walk up and down the hospital room, holding Daryl's head against my shoulder as he cried, my body instinctively *davening* like an old man in a synagogue.

After almost an hour of this, Bob stomped to the nurses' station, yelling so loud I could hear him. "It's ten o'clock," he hollered. "The operation was scheduled for nine. What the hell is going on?"

"Dr. Siegal is running a little behind today," the head nurse said patiently. "He should be here any minute."

"Don't you people have the brains to give a baby first priority?" Bob boomed.

"I'm sorry, sir," the nurse said, her voice now icy, "but we have other patients who deserve priority too."

I cringed; while I felt that Bob's behavior was justified, I was mortified by the way he alienated hospital staff. A pattern was established: me, all compliant helplessness; he, all fury and—mostly ineffectual—action.

Finally they took Daryl into surgery, and we sat down to wait. During the three-hour operation, we did crossword puzzles together; sometimes I read women's magazines. We didn't talk except to consult about puzzle clues. Not once did I think about what was transpiring downstairs; I clipped recipes and drank coffee, and received the news that my baby had survived with the same emotional expression with which I'd perused *Redbook's Budget Cookbook for Rainy Days*.

How to explain my apparent insouciance? I suppose that witnessing the insertion of needles into my baby's scalp and holding him while his stomach clutched with hunger pangs had been quite enough, thank you. I was learning how to tune out. I was learning how to survive as the mother of a chronically ill child.

Don't ask me what Bob was feeling—if I didn't face my own struggle, how could I begin to comprehend his? All I know is that in the next few months he developed a strange tic in his neck, while I, formerly an enthusiastic eater on a perpetual diet, dropped to ninety-five pounds.

Daryl came home, and I resumed the task of caring for him. Still he threw up, and I washed out his clothes. Still he cried most of the night, and I wheeled him up and down in a carriage. Still his head grew, and the doctor pushed on his bulging fontanel. He instructed us to have Daryl sleep in an upright position, as if this were standard therapy for hydrocephalus. We concocted a vertical bed from an infant seat, put the seat in a carriage, and rocked. Daryl soon developed breathing problems and chronic constipation. Following some sort of instinct, I exercised his legs a few times a day, but I was afraid to defy the doctor's orders, to let him lie down too long for fear the fluid would accumulate in his head. My ribs ached; I couldn't eat; I washed, fed, rocked.

There is something terribly wrong with a society that makes no provision for such a situation, don't you think? I wondered if it was different elsewhere. I'd read that in post-Mao China, people lived communally and had universal health care. I wondered how, when a baby with hydrocephalus was born into the community, it was handled. Maybe one of their famous "foot doctors" came around to explain to the parents—no, to the entire commune-what hydrocephalus was, and what could be done about it. I imagined a support group alternating work shifts to help care for the baby and reassure the parents. I imagined parents of children with hydrocephalus being put in contact with each other. Perhaps in a more humane society two young people weren't forced to assume the entire burden alone.

But knowing what I know now about China, and about the treatment of people with disabilities everywhere, it's more likely that they drown babies born with hydrocephalus.

"I don't know how you do it," Sylvia marveled. She came over once a week and taught me how to cook Bob's favorite dishes. The kitchen would grow redolent with the aroma of Russian stuffed cabbage or chicken fricassee, while Daryl watched us from his infant seat in the carriage. Every so often I'd leave the stove to squeeze Quacksie, a yellow plastic duck that honked loudly and made Daryl giggle.

"What wuzzat?" I'd chortle, delighted when he laughed and clapped his hands.

"You're wonderful," Sylvia said, giving me some badly needed strokes—but she always added a phrase I would often hear: "I don't know how you do it."

What does it mean for someone to say, "I don't know how you do it"? To me it sounded as if they saw themselves far removed from my world; the statement placed me beyond the pale of everyday human experience. It told me that they could not begin to imagine themselves in my place—when the truth is, any accident could have pushed anyone into my situation—and they, like me, would endure.

"You do what you have to do," I shrugged.

It never occurred to me to ask for help. Even when the county public nurse came calling, I pretended to need nothing. After all, whenever I'd heard about a new mother being "unable to cope," she was roundly condemned as weak and immature, qualities I did not particularly want to be known for. I did visit the doctor regularly with complaints of the pain in my ribs, headaches, and other psychosomatic symptoms, none of which he or I connected to stress.

Also, I was trying to appear normal at all costs. This meant that, in conversations about babies, I remained silent.

"This kid's driving me nuts now that she's crawling—she pokes her fingers into the outlets, she gets into everything," a mother would complain.

I clucked in false sympathy; my baby couldn't crawl.

"Why do you have those cushions on your infant seat?" someone would ask.

"He sleeps in it."

"He sleeps sitting up?"

"It's to drain spinal fluid."

She'd look at me queerly, or else look away, embarrassed.

One friend, Barbara, was the only exception; unlike most everyone else, she was matter-of-fact and accepting of Daryl's condition. Maybe it was because her mother worked in a pharmacy, so she'd been raised on talk of illness and cures all her life; at any rate, she seemed to view Daryl's situation as just another medical challenge.

"My mother says you should try a vaporizer for his breathing," she'd report. "And she says you shouldn't feel bad that he has to sleep sitting up because he's a baby and doesn't know anything else."

When Barbara's son turned a year old she invited several of our old friends and their babies to his party. I looked forward to seeing people I hadn't seen since high school graduation, and was especially eager to see Tommy, my old bowling partner.

"Hey bro," I said, standing on my toes to give him a kiss. "How goes it?"

"Okay," he mumbled quickly, turning his attention away from me.

I felt hurt, but told myself that he was probably afraid his wife would be jealous—hell, Bob was none too happy today, confronted by a couple of my old boyfriends.

But later on, after the birthday cake, I was feeding Daryl his bottle when I glanced up and caught Tommy, who was sitting across the table from me, casting sidelong glances at Daryl's head. I was stung.

That was the last my old high school friends saw of me.

Like many children with hydrocephalus, Daryl compensated for slow physical growth with a near-genius level of verbal development. Though he couldn't sit up unassisted until nearly a year, at seven months he was reciting song lyrics and nursery rhymes with stunning accuracy. Our days were full of music, and we chattered constantly to one another. I read him Shakespeare along with Dr. Seuss and performed *Funny Girl* and *West Side Story*; he giggled and applauded my theatrics. He was the best companion—not to mention audience—I'd ever had.

Still his head grew, he threw up, he cried at night: the shunt wasn't working. The neurosurgeon had begun to quake visibly whenever we walked into his office. Finally he admitted defeat and sent us to a pediatric neurosurgeon in New York who specialized in hydrocephalus.

Dr. Abrams was a short stocky man with a mass of dark curls atop his owl-shaped head. His eyeglasses were so thick I imagined slicing cheese on them. After examining Daryl, he told us that the shunt wasn't working, had probably never worked. He advised putting in a new one immediately.

"And oh," he told us, "let him lie down to sleep." His lips pursed together tightly as he added with a deep sigh, "Please."

"Parents with children who are repeatedly hospitalized experience post-traumatic shock. When their child gets sick or is rehospitalized, the parents relive the trauma of previous stays and often feel like they themselves have sustained a visceral wound."
—from *Special Kids Need Special Parents*

A Resource for Parents of Children with Special Needs
—By Judith Loseff Lavin

3

The Road Gets Rougher

A photograph. My mother sits, her face wreathed in smiles, holding a frothy cake up to the camera, on which is written "Welcome Home Daryl." Beside her stands a young woman, hair teased high, smiling so fiercely any idiot can see she's faking it, holding in her thin arms a baby whose large head, shaven on one side, droops over her elbow; the baby's face is a study in fatigue. Daryl has just returned home after his second operation.

For Bob and I, whose short lives had been spent almost entirely in suburbia, the huge university-affiliated hospital was something of a culture shock; perhaps the closest parallel in my experience had been Kennedy Airport.

People of all nationalities scurried about with attaché cases and clipboards; wheeled vehicles of all kinds rolled through the halls; the main floor was a city unto itself with administrative offices, a gift shop, luncheonette, cafeteria, and huge waiting rooms furnished with salmon-colored plastic sofas. Bells clanged; loudspeakers called urgently for doctors; beepers rang out from jacket pockets. Beneath an olio of women's perfume wafted an indefinable smell, the hospital's own distinctive odor.

After an interview in the admitting room, we were escorted to an elevator; as we stepped inside, two orderlies entered, pushing a sleeping man on a stretcher. The patient's arm was hooked to a pole from which hung a bag of yellowish fluid. Unnerved, I stared fixedly up at the lighted floor numbers. A small sign over the "5" read, "No Visitors on Fifth Floor." I imagined secret horrific torture chambers; later I learned that the fifth floor housed the hospital's operating rooms.

While Bob went off to handle insurance forms, a nurse ushered Daryl and me into a room overlooking the East River.

"I'm Nurse Simon, head of pediatrics," she told me. "I'd like to ask you a few questions. Why don't you just put the baby into the crib."

"He needs to be changed," I said, feeling inexplicably apologetic for this inconvenience.

As I removed his wet diaper, the nurse leaned over and clucked, "Hello, Daryl.'

Daryl's eyes lit up; he waved his arms excitedly. "Hi," he said happily. "Hi."

"What a bright baby!"

I beamed, accustomed to such remarks. But when the nurse took out her notebook and began questioning me, I instinctively felt as if I were being tested.

"Is he allergic to any foods?"

"Not that I know of."

"What foods does he particularly like or dislike?"

Like or dislike? I fed him baby food, all varieties; he wasn't a great eater. I had never considered that he might have preferences—he was, after all, just a baby. I shoveled in the strained carrots or beef and cleaned up whatever he spat out.

"I'm not sure," I answered, feeling like an imbecile.

"Well, what does he eat?"

"Cereal, mashed bananas, the usual. He's not a big eater."

The nurse checked something on her chart. "Does he have any favorite toys?"

On more secure territory, I pulled Quacksie out of my diaper bag and squeezed. Daryl giggled. Nurse Simon smiled with polite indulgence.

"Does he have any difficulty moving his bowels?"

"He gets constipated a lot."

"Then why do you feed him bananas?"

"Huh?"

"Bananas are an extremely binding food."

"Binding?"

"Constipating." She seemed impatient with me.

"I didn't know that," I said sheepishly.

The nurse did not comment, but continued down her list. Rashes? Vomiting? Does he sleep well at night? I answered, telling myself it was all just part of the hospital routine, but I felt like I was being examined in Motherhood 101—and failing.

"The doctor will be making his rounds shortly," Nurse Simon said, closing her notebook. "Visiting hours for parents are 11:00 until 7:00."

"Eleven to seven?" I was so stunned I didn't even try to hide my dismay.

Nurse Simon's head jerked up from her notes. Slowly she removed her glasses and looked at me directly for the first time.

"I mean," I stammered, "in the other hospital we were only allowed to visit for two hours a day."

"We believe it's better for the children," she said, "to have their parents with them as much as possible. Is that a problem for you, Mrs.—" she consulted her notes—"Mrs. H?"

"No, of course not," I said, my words coming out in a long exhalation. "In fact, I'm glad, it was so hard the other time..." I broke off. The truth was, Daryl's earlier hospitalization had provided me a badly needed respite from the initial shock of motherhood.

"Well," said Nurse Simon, putting her glasses back on and fixing me with a thoughtful gaze, "You should be very happy with this arrangement."

I got the message: I wasn't just *allowed* to be at the hospital all day, I was *expected* to be.

Nurse Simon had just left the room when Bob stomped in, flinging a stack of insurance papers onto the bureau. "They're not gonna start testing until Monday," he said, walking over to the window and staring out, his arms folded across his massive chest, his legs apart in a soldier's stance. "They don't do tests over the weekend."

"Then how come they told us to check in on Friday?"

"Probably for the insurance money. The bastards."

"Hallo." A small dark man wearing a white turban stuck his head in the doorway. "May I come in?" Before we could respond, he came forward, hand outstretched to shake Bob's.

"I am Dr. Kayim, the house doctor. May I examine the patient?"

Again, he didn't wait for a response. As he poked Daryl's stomach, listened to his heart and wiggled his legs, he asked us questions. Do either of you have a family history of diabetes? Tuberculosis? Heart trouble? Any siblings?

Bob and I answered, having great difficulty understanding Dr. Kayim. I had never seen a Pakistani person before, much less spoken to one. In the coming weeks I was to converse with more people of different nationalities than I'd seen in my entire life; well, converse is not really the word: I was to repeat the answers to the same questions, about diabetes and heart murmurs, over and over to Indians, Pakistanis, Japanese, Chinese. If I was intimidated by people of my own culture when they donned the white coat of medical authority, these foreigners totally terrified me. I felt like a random target: anyone who passed the room seemed to feel it incumbent upon them to enter and probe into my life.

After Dr. Kayim left, Daryl fell asleep and I read magazines. An hour passed. Two. Dinner was wheeled around. The room darkened. Bob fell asleep. Just as I felt I would scream from sheer boredom, Dr. Abrams, surrounded by a coterie of five or six medical students, swooshed through the door in a flurry of white.

"Bob. Mrs. H." He nodded perfunctorily, marched directly to the crib, let down the sidebar, and held a newly awakened Daryl in a sitting position. The students gathered round, staring at Daryl through their thick eyeglasses.

"Here's a case of congenital hydrocephalus," Dr. Abrams began. "Here the skull, as you can see, is asymmetrical." He cradled Daryl's head as if it were a sculpture by Rodin, turning it this way and that for his students' inspection.

"Very unusual," one of the students noted, scribbling on a pad.

"A ventriculo-atrial shunt was inserted two weeks after birth." Dr. Abrams ran a forefinger down the hairless shuntline on the side of Daryl's head. He pushed on the fontanel, frowning in concentration. He pulled out a tape and measured Daryl's head, describing the failure of the shunt and the operation he would perform next week. The students leaned progressively closer, peering at the baby with the big head.

Daryl thought they were playing with him; he chattered, laughed and grabbed at the doctor's glasses until he was forced to put them into his pocket.

"I don't believe this," I said, looking towards Bob in a frank appeal that he slay these monsters, or at least chase them away from my baby.

With a great sigh of resignation, Bob hoisted himself from his chair and tugged at his pants, which had as usual fallen below his pot belly. "Dr. Abrams," he said coldly, "can I see you for a second?"

"Why sure, Bob, we're just finishing up."

Bob followed the white brigade out into the hall. When he returned, his pants had fallen below his belly again and his shoulders were slumped in defeat.

"He says it's part of the routine, that's why this is such a great hospital—the students learn from the patients." He lifted Daryl out of the crib. "How ya doin', tough guy? Did those guys make you feel like a monkey?" Daryl pulled on Bob's thick lips and giggled. "Mon-key."

I watched Bob holding his problematic son, so tiny in his huge arms. Despite everything, Bob adored Daryl. Occasionally I wondered—with good cause, as it turned out—what would happen when reality forced him to stop referring to his son as "tough guy," but for now he turned to me and said, "You know, babe, he's a perfect person."

For one brief moment the sounds of the hospital gurneys receded, the odor of disinfectant vanished. There was no shunt, no big head, no vomiting. There was only this perfect little person.

Daryl stuck his hands into Bob's curly black hair and pulled.

"Hey, you shouldda done that to those doctors," Bob laughed as he pried Daryl's little fingers from his hair. "Better yet, you should have poked out one of their eyes."

"Or peed in their faces," I giggled, "like he does to me!"

"Did you see that little creep with the red hair?" Bob asked. "He must be some kind of neck fetishist—he kept checking the size and color of Daryl's neck."

"We're terrible," I said, still giggling. "After all, they're trying to help kids like Daryl."

"Yeah," Bob agreed, with little conviction.

The five-hour operation was performed on Wednesday morning. Dr. Abrams reopened the four-inch scar on the side of Daryl's head, and made an incision in the neck. He removed the faulty shunt and inserted a new one. Then he sewed everything back together, and Daryl was wheeled to his room with his half-shaven head turbaned in white. Dr. Abrams gave me the old shunt, a small plastic tube resembling a ballpoint pen refill, as a souvenir.

We sat beside Daryl as he slept. His cheeks were rosy—a sign, I thought, of rapid recovery, but later learned was a side effect of anesthesia. I sat silently while Bob kept up an active vigil—checking to see that the IV was dripping, raising the pillow half an inch, leaning down to listen to Daryl's breathing. All these acts were completely meaningless; there was nothing, in actuality, we could do for our son. He was in the hands of the medical profession, and we had little choice but to put our faith in them. So while Bob seized an illusory control, I retreated once more into the *Ladies' Home Journal*.

By the next day Daryl was completely alert; he carried on conversations with the nurses and aides, becoming a favorite patient.

Bob returned to work, while I spent long days in the hospital, wandering from lounge to cafeteria to Daryl's room, playing with him, doing crossword puzzles, reading magazines. The hospital world became, for me, more real than the one outside: when I did go out I found myself blinking at traffic lights, viewing the scurrying pedestrians and frantic drivers as deluded for taking their trivial activities so seriously. The hospital was real; the concerns of the people in it were serious; all else was folly.

At first I tried going home each night; it was nearly a two-hour drive, during which I worried that something might happen to Daryl and I'd be unreachable. Once home, I'd find myself wandering from room to room, not knowing what to do with myself.

The hospital had a two-bed "mother's room," but there was an endless waiting list to get in. At that time there was no such thing as a McDonalds's House or any other accommodations for parents of hospitalized children. The only person who lived in Manhattan who I knew well enough to ask for a bed was my grandfather.

I sat on his blue plastic-covered sofa politely sipping the hot chocolate that Bertha, my grandfather's third wife, had made for me. The TV volume was turned up to accommodate his hearing loss; canned laughter from "My Mother The Car" ricocheted like machine gun fire off the walls of the one-room hotel apartment.

Great Benny, as my niece had dubbed our family patriarch, sat in a stuffed armchair puffing on a Cuban cigar, despite the fact that a small tumor had been recently removed from his lung. He was either going mad from fear of death, which came two years later, or just plain senile. Over the loud television he shouted stories at me, family stories of skeletons in the closet along with opinions as to the sanity of other relatives.

I recalled sitting on his lap, a child of five, squealing with delight as he squeezed my buttocks and tickled my neck with wet kisses. Just a few weeks ago he had, but gingerly, held Daryl, not squeezing or kissing him.

By the time "H-e-r-e-s Johnny" echoed off the walls, my brain was numb. My grandfather was still weaving stories through artful smoke rings, seemingly ready to talk all night. Bertha, who chided him affectionately, finally noticed my glazed eyes and opened up the sofa bed. As I drifted off to sleep I heard her whispering to him.

The next morning Great Benny took me to a Greek coffee shop for breakfast before walking me to the hospital, where he apologized for his inability to visit Daryl. "I can't stand to see sick kids," he explained.

As we stood in front of the revolving glass doors, he pulled his wallet from his breast pocket, a gesture with which I was familiar. I expected the usual ten or twenty, but he thrust two fifties into my hand. "For a hotel," he said. "Bertha's a special kind of woman, you know. She can't sleep in the same room with strangers."

He planted a sloppy kiss on my cheek and hurried away in the morning mist.

That night, and most nights thereafter, I slept on a sofa in the lounge. Well, slept is a euphemism: in between long bouts of insomnia, I catnapped. I lay on the sofa, using my purse as a pillow and my coat as a blanket, and gazed out at the twinkling lights of Manhattan. Muted sounds drifted down the hall: the padded footsteps of a nurse, the squeaking of wheels, the whoosh of air as the ward doors opened. A father might enter the darkened room and quietly smoke by the window; a couple might sit in a corner whispering. Occasionally I heard the sound of weeping.

Later, in the depths of the night, an odd elevator beep would awaken me, and recapturing sleep would be impossible. I'd sit up and light a cigarette, staring out the window, drawing my coat around me in the now unheated room. Sometimes I'd turn on the fluorescent lights and read. Most often, though, I would walk.

Down to the basement, where I roamed the endless maze of hallways, nodding to workers who stacked linens or washed floors. Some of them nodded back, others looked at me curiously, but none were suspicious: American hospitals had not yet been forced to institute security measures.

I passed empty classrooms and briefly fantasized going to medical school. I discovered a meditation room where I began what would become a lifelong habit of stretching exercises. I wandered into the twenty-four-hour cafeteria where medical students conferred about patients while I sipped muddy coffee and watched the sun rise over the East River. Hospital staff came to recognize me, but they respected the aura of privacy I carefully cultivated.

Night after night I dozed and roamed, roamed and dozed. During the day I amused Daryl by squeezing Quacksie or playing games; when he napped or was taken for X-rays I sat in the waiting room.

My parents came to visit one evening, and Bob's sister came once as well. Other than that, I had no personal interactions with anyone other than Bob, who came for a few hours every couple of days. Whenever he arrived, I would feel a tremendous weight lift from my shoulders: someone to share the responsibility. But this relief was short-lived.

"Did Dr. Abrams come around yet today?" he'd ask me.

"Uh, I'm not sure."

"You're not sure? Don't you talk to him every day?"

"Um, not really."

Bob would look at me like I was mentally defective, and stomp out to the nurse's station to find out when Dr. Abrams would make his rounds.

"What did he eat today?"

"Applesauce and cereal."

"That's it?"

"He doesn't seem to like those undiluted meats they serve here." At least I'd learned he had definite culinary tastes.

"Why didn't you tell me? I could have brought some of the kind he likes." He pulled a twenty from his wallet. "Here. Go out and get something he'll eat." He turned away from me. "Hey tough guy. You don't like liver, huh? Don't worry, Daddy never did either and look how big he grew up to be."

The pediatric ward did not lack for loquacious mothers eager to pounce on the nearest available ear, but my guardedness kept most of them at bay. One particularly oblivious woman, however, managed to catch my attention.

Ellen Meyerhoff, a freckled frosted blonde in her early twenties introduced herself and, without any encouragement from me, launched into her story. Her two-year-old son had been operated on for a hole in his heart. Confident he'd be fine, Ellen felt she could now turn her energy to proper discipline.

"He's trying to get me to hold him all the time," she said, wrinkling a nose that had clearly been bobbed, "pretending it hurts. But he can't fool me. I just left him in the bed crying. I won't spoil him, no way. I don't want him using his operation to manipulate people. I'm going to make sure he grows up perfectly normal." She paused, took a compact from her expensive leather purse, and began applying mascara. "What's your son in for?"

"Hydrocephalus." My tongue still tripped awkwardly over the syllables.

"What's that?"

"It's when spinal fluid accumulates in the head..."

"Oh, water on the brain."

"Yeah," I said, flinching.

"We're going home tomorrow," said Ellen, now powdering her face, "and let me tell you, I cannot wait. I hate being in the city. I hate shopping here. Where I live, I can get into my car, park, come out with a bunch of bags, put them in the trunk and drive home. Here I gotta *schlep* everything around." She snapped her compact shut. A mega sized diamond flashed from her hand.

After that I assiduously avoided conversations, but one day I was caught off guard when an older woman plopped into the seat beside me. She was dressed in a beige suit, nylons and high heels; her tasteful pearl necklace exactly matched her earrings, and her hair had obviously been styled at a salon. She looked like one of those competent women who move mountains for their children and hold up the world with their pinkies.

"You're Daryl's mom, right?" she asked.

I quickly eyed her up and down, searching for an identifying badge: was she another social worker? I'd been approached by one the day before, a young fresh-faced girl who'd plied me with questions about my emotional condition in much the same tone as the doctors probed my medical history.

"How do you know?" I asked.

"Simple observation—I've seen you in his room. I read all the names on the doorways," she added with a laugh. "It alleviates the boredom. I'm Janet, by the way—Sandy's mom." She stuck out her hand for shaking. Limply I took it in mine and introduced myself, not having the foggiest notion who Sandy was.

"Daryl has hydrocephalus, doesn't he? Abrams is his doctor," she added quickly, "so I figured it out. Believe me, when you've been around hospitals as long as I have, everything becomes a source of fascination."

"What's your daughter here for?"

"A shunt revision, same as Daryl. It's her eighth."

I nearly dropped my magazine. "Her eighth?"

"She has spina bifida."

"Oh," I said, instantly relieved. I had heard of spina bifida: children who suffered from it not only had hydrocephalus, but were also paralyzed from the waist down. Sandy was obviously much more severely handicapped than Daryl, who would go home after this operation and live a perfectly normal life. Surely Janet and I had nothing in common.

"How old is Sandy?" I asked, just to be polite.

"Five."

Five years old, I thought; eight operations. No, Janet and I had nothing in common.

"Would you be interested in coming to a meeting?" she asked.

"What kind of meeting?"

"We've organized a group of parents of children with spina bifida. We meet once a month. Sometimes we invite speakers, like Dr. Abrams, or psychologists. It really helps."

"I don't know. Daryl only has hydrocephalus."

Janet raised her eyebrows and smiled, her lipsticked mouth turning into a shiny red bow. "That's not enough for you?"

"Well, I mean, I'm not sure we have the same problems."

"How old is Daryl?" she asked, taking my hand in hers.

"Eight months," I replied, gently pulling my hand away.

"Eight months. When Sandy was that age..." She broke off, searching my face, and seemed to decide not to say anymore. "Look, I'll just give you the information, and if you think you'd like to come, do. No obligation."

I took the scrap of paper, shoved it in my bag, and excused myself. In the privacy of the ladies' room I fumed. Where did this woman get off asking me to join up with parents of kids with spina bifida? Those kids were severely handicapped, living in wheelchairs. Shit, I didn't belong with them. Sure, Daryl had all that trouble in the beginning, but that was because of that stupid doctor on Long Island. Now that the operation had been done right, he'd recover, and we would go home to live a normal life.

For that is how I viewed life when I was younger: as a series of disconnected events having no bearing upon each other. Daryl was sick now, but would soon be well. We were in a hospital now, but would soon leave it behind. At nineteen, I could see no connection between past, present and future, no repercussions arising from Daryl's condition.

Ergo, a welcome home celebration for Daryl—who, I am sure, wanted nothing more than to lie in his crib with Quacksie by his side.

4

Denial

After Daryl's second operation, there was no more projectile vomiting, no more sleepless nights. But still a fear gnawed at me, a dread that I would do something wrong—bump his head, say, and throw the shunt out of whack. Or perhaps he'd cut his scalp somehow and there would be a violent outpouring of thick yellowish fluid. Maybe he'd die, and Bob, who monitored every move I made with his son, would blame me.

The nasty underside of my fear revealed itself in nightmares—dreams in which Daryl's little limbs lay scattered about, his head severed from his torso. Dreams of throwing him out the window, watching his head crack and splatter on the pavement. Having had a rudimentary education in Freudian psychology, I wondered if these dreams were merely nightmares, or wishes arising from my subconscious.

I had no way of knowing that many mothers have these kinds of dreams and fantasies; certainly nobody in my suburban community talked about them, and even today, this isn't exactly a popular topic of discussion.

The censorship of negative feelings—which in my case were predictably strong—actually led to their subconscious enactment: Daryl's early years were fraught with a series of "accidents." There was the time I took him out of the sink after a bath and banged his head on the overhead cabinet. And the time I watched distractedly as his cousin inadvertently crushed Daryl's toe beneath the rocking chair. Most serious was when I jerked him to a standing position and his head fell back onto the curbstone, necessitating three stitches in his forehead.

We'd be playing: I'd tickle and squeeze him, laughing with pleasure, when my laughter suddenly turned to rage and my tickles became sadistic pinches. I did always stop short of really hurting him.

The truth? To have thrown him out the window or strangled him with my bare hands would have given me, momentarily at least, a deep sense of satisfaction. To annihilate the source of so much fear, anxiety, and tedium would have granted me sublime pleasure. To simply be rid of him: to divorce his father and leave that ridiculous life I'd never chosen, seemed like the ultimate relief. I understand mothers who abuse or kill their offspring; I have never believed that Medea acted solely out of revenge towards Jason.

Bob somehow got wind of the spina bifida group and wanted to go to a meeting. Reluctantly I agreed.

About fifty couples sat before the evening's speaker, a pediatric psychologist. He was a plump, affable man who opened the lecture, much to my alarm, with a variation on the ethnic joke.

"Of all the troubles with which we Jews have been afflicted," he began, "spina bifida does not seem to rank with the top ten. For no discernible reason, the percentage of Jews with this disease is relatively small."

I gazed around the room seeking other Jews, but it was impossible to tell. So, not only was I defective as a mother, but I had also brought an anomalous *shanda* into the tribe of Israel. I looked to Bob to see if he felt as I did; his neck was twitching, but his face unreadable.

"But there is a sensibility," the speaker continued, "which Jews bring to this issue—the sensibility of a discriminated-against minority."

My ears perked up: this was the first I'd heard anyone speak of the handicapped as discriminated-against. It was a concept that filled me with a feeling I could not yet define, something akin to hope. As the psychologist spoke about societal attitudes towards children with dis-abilities, I remembered the man who, passing us in a shopping mall, had pointed to Daryl and told his daughter, "That boy must be very smart, his head is so big." When I'd complained to my mother, who was with me, she'd told me I was "too sensitive," that the man had obviously intended it as a compliment.

During the discussion that followed, one woman related an incident when a passerby showered her son, who was in a wheelchair, with pity. "Here I am," she said, "trying to raise him as normally as possible, and this total stranger walks up and treats him like a freak. How do you deal with such people?"

"You've got to give these kids a strong sense of self-worth," said the psychologist, "stronger even than you'd give another child, so they'll be able to deal with society. They have to learn not to be affected by it."

My brief moment of hopefulness vanished; while the shrink had acknowledged social oppression, he hadn't gone so far as to suggest fighting against it. Once again, the responsibility rested squarely on parental shoulders.

But what of the perpetrators of insensitive behavior? I wondered. Should they remain immune to criticism or re-education? Can parents really raise their children in such a manner that society will never infringe upon their psyches? And if they fail, is it then the parents' fault?

These thoughts confused me, made me feel out of sync with the earnest mothers and fathers all around me. Slowly I distanced myself from the proceedings: they were, after all, talking about wheelchairs. Daryl would not have to use one, and his body, I had been assured, would eventually grow in proportion to his head. With time, no one need ever know he'd had hydrocephalus as an infant.

When the lecture ended, coffee and cake were served, and people talked animatedly in clusters; they even laughed a lot. Bob and I stood on the sidelines; I felt as isolated as I did at gatherings of "normal" parents, absurdly wishing that I fully belonged in this group.

"I'm so glad you came," said Janet, approaching our corner and extending her hand. I introduced her to Bob.

"What do you think?" she asked.

"It's interesting...but I still feel kind of...are there any groups of parents of kids with just hydrocephalus?"

"There you go again," Janet laughed. "Your wife," she said to Bob, "isn't content with just an excess of spinal fluid. She wants the whole bit or nothing."

Bob's jaw dropped.

"Oh, come on," Janet prodded. "If we can't laugh at our problems, we're sunk."

"I guess you've been dealing with this longer than we have," Bob conceded.

"You'll get used to it. Look, why don't you ask Dr. Abrams for some names of patients with hydrocephalus and call them yourself? As far as I know, there's no formal organization."

"It's odd that there isn't," I said. "I mean, he told us that 8000 kids a year are born with it."

"Yes, but look how new the operation is," Janet said, waving her hand through the air.

"What difference does that make?" Bob asked, genuinely bewildered.

"Well," said Janet, "our group only started a year ago."

Years later I realized that she was trying to tell us that there'd been no organization because there were no surviving children. She must have seen how naive and fragile we were, groping our way through the surreal world of doctors, hospitals, and the handicapped, and decided that we were not quite ready to hear that kind of information.

Dr. Abrams gave me a few names of parents of children with hydrocephalus, and I found two mothers who were eager to meet. We arranged a coffee klatch at one of their homes, with the children.

Dorothy Leoni came to the door wearing an apron and waving a chocolate covered plastic spatula in her hand. Her short curly hair was uncombed, and her eyes bulged over deep bags. She looked like she hadn't slept in a week.

"Come in, come in. You'll have to excuse me, I'm just putting the cookies in." She dashed into the kitchen, and I followed, carrying Daryl on my hip. The smell of Toll House cookies filled the air.

Seated in a high chair was two-year-old Rebecca, a big-eyed child with dark hair and skinny arms. I immediately noted that her head was about the same size as Daryl's, and though it wobbled a bit, she was sitting up by herself. Rebecca proved to be as bright and verbal as Daryl; in between putting cookies in and out of the oven Dorothy directed her to recite her repertoire of songs and rhymes. The second mother, Joanne, arrived with her four-year-old son Brian, who was wearing a football helmet.

"He falls down so much," she explained, frantically trying to light a cigarette: her matches, apparently damp, kept fizzling out. I handed her a lighter. "Thanks," she said, her eyes searching the living room for booby traps. "Once he cracked his shunt."

"What happened?" I asked, shocked.

"He had to have a new one put in. He's had four operations." She lunged forward to grab Brian as he was about to tumble off the sofa he'd managed to climb. He immediately scrambled out of her grasp and headed for an open window. Joanne dashed after him. For once I was glad that Daryl was safely ensconced in an infant seat.

Dorothy dominated the conversation with a blow-by-blow account of her daughter's surgery; I was relieved to learn that this child had had only one operation.

"It was two weeks before Christmas when she got out of the hospital. I had to buy presents for all four of my kids, bake my cookies, decorate my house, shop, cook, clean." She ticked off these items on the fingers of both hands. "Then I had Christmas Eve to get through, Christmas day with my husband's family from Vermont, and then

New Year's. Then came my oldest's birthday on the 2nd. So I had no time to get depressed. I thank Jesus Christ for helping me through."

I squirmed, trying to avoid looking at the many crucifixes nailed to the walls.

"Daryl was born in the summer," I began, but my voice stuck in my throat. I longed to talk about my experience, but after Dorothy's upbeat sermon I was afraid that my anger and confusion might come spilling out. Joanne was constantly in and out of the room, chasing after Brian. I found myself reacting as I had to Janet and the spina bifida group—as if we had nothing in common. Maybe we shared the identical situation, but we sure didn't share the same reactions to it.

Driving home, I decided that I probably wouldn't contact these women again. Their unsuitability was clear: Dorothy was religious; Joanne was neurotic. Under other circumstances, I told myself, I would not have sought them out as friends—so why allow the coincidence of hydrocephalus to draw us together?

I turned on the radio and hummed along with the Beatles while Daryl fell asleep in the back seat. Mentally I planned that night's dinner—a new recipe for chicken flambé from *Good Housekeeping*.

5

The Girl Who Ate with Her Toes

I sat in a corner helping Daryl pile up blocks, but it was difficult to stay focussed on what we were doing. In the center of the room a black girl of about ten was playing checkers with her feet. Armless, this was the only way she could play—but her skill with her toes was something to see. Her partner, a Chinese boy of about the same age, leaned forward on his butt: he had no legs. We were in a center adjacent to New York University Hospital, where children with disabilities were evaluated and given physical therapy. At eighteen months, Daryl was here to be evaluated.

Many of the children were thalidomide babies—those whose mothers had taken the drug during their pregnancies, before it was discovered that it produced children without limbs and with other deformities. I'd seen babies with stumps for arms, kids with all kinds of physical permutations, even some with hydeocephalus whose heads were far larger than Daryl's. I watched them crawl across the floor on their torsos, eat with their feet, lie down while therapists moved their shriveled legs. But the armless girl was by far the most fascinating: she did things with her legs, feet and toes that I couldn't do with four intact limbs. I began to wonder about the meaning of the word "normal." In this place she was, if anything, supernormal, a subject for admiration.

But when I went home at night, leaving Daryl there with these children, my lofty ideas about normalcy and superhuman skills vanished. I dreamt Technicolor Fellini-esque freak shows filled with alien diaboli-cal creatures. I worried about their effect on my child, staying in the place for ten days. Was he frightened? Would he be scarred for life?

Not to worry. Daryl, as always, endeared himself to the staff with his command of the English language. Apparently he was unfazed by the so-called "freaks" around him. Years later I would attribute his accep-tance of people with disabilities and other oddballs to his childhood experience.

Nonetheless, I was relieved when he came home. From the evalua-tion we learned that he had suffered some brain damage from the hydrocephalus, which would manifest itself in perceptual disabilities. Unable to accurately gauge shapes, sizes and their relationships to each other, he couldn't do simple puzzles, A long report detailed the kinds of tasks he'd have trouble with in school—but no advice as to how to change any of it.

Today, we would have been taught exercises to mitigate the effects of perceptual problems. Daryl might have received early intervention from physical therapists. At that time, however, all the medical system had to offer was to prepare us for what to expect, not what to do about it.

When Daryl was a teenager he got a job mowing a neighbor's lawn. It didn't last very long, because he left huge swatches of grass uncut; he was unable to distinguish where he was going with the lawn mower, or which areas he had already cut. This was the most tangible instance of how his perceptual disability affected his actions—but many of the problems he had throughout his formal education, I now realize, can be attributed to this.

Probably the biggest deprivation resulting from Daryl's perceptual disability is that he cannot drive a car. When he was sixteen I paid for him to get driving lessons, but he so terrified the instructors that they refused to continue teaching him. For years he still fantasized driving, and only gave up the dream some time in his late twenties. Doomed to public transportation, he resents this every day of his life. Oddly enough, he's an expert at recognizing various makes of automobiles, and hangs pictures of snazzy cars all over his walls.

For me Daryl's inability to drive is comparable to his being two and a half before he was able to walk, so I had to carry him everywhere—even when I had a second child on my hip. In this case, I must drive him wherever public transportation doesn't go—including to visit me. Like most older mothers, I love it when my son comes over for dinner, but he can only come if I pick him up and drive him home—and the older I get the more I loathe fighting traffic, driving at night, in the rain, anywhere really. Given the possibilities of what Daryl could have suffered as an adult, this is, admittedly, a small inconvenience. Were I a better person I would dismiss it and thank God things aren't worse.

But I am not a better person, and I still don't believe in God.

6

A Homecoming

I was on my hands and knees scrubbing the bathroom tiles when Bob walked in on me.

"What the hell are you doing?" he asked, taking his penis out to pee.

"Cleaning."

"You're scrubbing the tiles with a toothbrush. What's gotten into you?"

"Don't you remember? Angie's coming over today."

Bob grunted. He had never liked Angie. For a long time I'd thought his animosity derived from her rejection of him when he'd made a pass at her back in high school; she'd gone out with his best friend instead. Later on I realized he was jealous of our closeness; when she'd gone to Japan to get married I'd sobbed inconsolably, but when he went off to the National Guard I'd barely shed a tear.

"Will you be home in time to see her?" I asked, hoping the answer would be no.

"I don't think so," he said gruffly, buckling his belt and tucking in his crisp work shirt. "I have a couple of appointments tonight."

"Well, okay, I'll tell her you said hello."

He left the bathroom and I continued scrubbing. Luckily, I'd cleaned the rest of the house the day before, and had made tuna fish salad for lunch. Most of my morning would be devoted to making myself look as much like my old self as possible.

I opened the door, feeling a mixture of caution and anticipation. Before me stood the girl who'd been my closest friend throughout high school, holding a dimpled cherub of ten months on one small hip. We laughed simultaneously, then moved into an awkward embrace, baby Darlene giggling and pulling on my hair.

"Hello there!" I exclaimed, appraising the baby, who gurgled. "She's adorable," I said. "Come in, come in."

I led her into the kitchen where Daryl sat in his carriage infant seat, playing with Quacksie. "Who's this?" Angie gushed, placing Darlene on the floor by her feet. The child immediately pulled herself onto all fours. She resembled, I thought, a tadpole, as she slid across the checkered linoleum. Angie tickled Daryl's neck. "I'm your Aunt Angie," she told him.

"An-gie!" he said, smiling and waving his arms around excitedly.

"I don't believe it! He said my name already! Darlene only knows how to say Mama."

Darlene had made her way over to the cabinets and was tugging on a knob. The door opened.

"You don't have locks on your cabinets?" Angie asked incredulously.

"I haven't needed them yet," I said, my face flushing.

"I'll have to watch her every second,"Angie moaned. "She gets into everything. Get over here," she said brusquely, swooping Darlene into her arms. The child fought to be let down, but Angie held fast. "She drives me crazy, she's into everything in the house," Angie said.

I tried to appear sympathetic and understanding but, given that Daryl couldn't crawl, I hadn't experienced this phase of motherhood yet—and fervently wished I had.

Angie had brought an infant seat, which she put Darlene in for lunch. We fed the babies, making small talk. Never had Angie and I been so distant, talking about the weather, my apartment, old friends she wanted to visit. Always, we had cut right to the chase, confiding intimate details of our lives. After the kids were fed and we placed them in the playpen in front of the television, we sat face to face at my kitchen table. There were no more distractions. I wished there were.

"Do you want to tell me about it?" she asked, lighting a cigarette and holding my eyes with hers. I stared into those same green pools that I knew as well as my own face, thinking how beautiful she was, those big eyes lighting up the olive skin around them, her lush berry red lips now in repose, not smiling or chortling to the babies. I had never ceased to be almost hypnotized by the beauty of that face.

"About what?" I asked, looking away.

"About what! Daryl. The operations. The hydroencephitlus."

"Hydrocephalus," I corrected automatically.

"Whatever. I know you been hurtin'."

I stood and walked to the sink, stalling, filling a glass with water. "Do you want anything to drink?"

"Marcy, get your ass into that chair and talk to me."

I sat down, defeated. "Well, there's not so much to tell. He had his last operation a few months ago and he seems to be doing okay. With any luck he's going to live a normal life."

"But tell me what it's been *like*," she prodded.

I opened my mouth, then shut it again. I looked down at my hands, traced a line of sugar on the cool formica table.

"Come on, Marce. Barbara must have told you about my letters, what a hard time I had when Dar was born."

Barbara had told me: With barely disguised contempt she'd detailed Angie's sleepless nights with a colicky baby, her loneliness, her feelings of inadequacy. "I wish she'd stop being such a baby," Barbara had said. "She's a mother now, she needs to grow up."

These judgements had the effect of making me conceal my own ambivalence about motherhood from Barbara. I wondered, though, why Angie hadn't confessed all this in her letters to me. As if reading my mind now, she said, "I didn't complain so much to you—I figured you had it worse than me."

"You should have," I said, surprising myself. "I would have felt better knowing someone else wasn't a happy perfect mother."

At this she laughed, a sound without mirth, full of irony and bitterness. "You're right, I should have told you. I guess I just wanted to talk to you in person. You know I was in labor over twenty-six hours? When I called my mother and told her it hurt, she said 'what'd you 'speck?'" Angie's perfect intonation of her mother's Italian accent brought to mind a vivid picture of the tiny silver-haired woman. "I mean, the woman had seven kids," Angie continued. For the next half hour she chain-smoked and talked, relating her labor in minute detail, her first night alone with the baby, and subsequent nights when she tried in vain to comfort a very unhappy Darlene. "I felt so alone, and so helpless," she said. "I'm glad to be home."

I sat mesmerized, as always, asking encouraging questions, nodding in agreement, laughing at her rueful stories. I was glad to be off the hot seat, not to have to tell her my story. She had always been able to captivate my interest, even when talking about the most mundane topics. It was partly her face, so beautiful and so changeable, that held me; it was also the way she spoke, straight from the heart, so different from the way that most people talked. That voice washed over me, bathing me in love and emotion, offering a space to reciprocate.

But I did not reciprocate. I simply could not begin to tell anyone, not even Angie, the painful truth about Daryl's infancy. On some level I was ashamed to introduce so much misery into a situation—motherhood—that was supposed to be glorious. It didn't matter that Angie didn't think it was all so glorious: I was hung up in my own self-judgment, afraid of receiving hers.

She was telling me about her flight from Japan when a loud wail rose up from the living room, and we both stood automatically and ran inside. Darlene was standing up, holding the playpen netting, bouncing up and down on chubby legs. When she saw Angie, she lifted her arms and wailed louder to be let out. Angie sighed and reached for her. Daryl sat quietly, watching this mini-drama with interest.

I lifted him out of the playpen and strapped him into his carriage. Angie put Darlene on the floor. She immediately scampered on all fours towards the bathroom. "Damn, now we can't talk," Angie said, following the baby's trail.

I sat down on the sofa and gazed at Daryl, content to sit confined in his usual position. Waves of envy washed over me: I wished he could crawl around like Darlene. `

"No!" I heard Angie shriek from inside. "Bad girl." I got up and went to see what was going on: Darlene had grabbed a can of Comet from the bathtub and was sprinkling it liberally around the floor and herself. Angie dove down to take it away from her. I laughed. "She's so cute," I said jealously.

"Cute, huh? You're lucky you don't have to deal with this."

I turned quickly and headed back to the living room, stung to the core. Lucky? How could she be so insensitive? I wrapped my pain around me like a protective shawl; so, Angie was just like everyone else—totally unaware of what I was going through. Never mind that I'd refused to tell her: she should have guessed. "Fuck em all," I muttered to myself, then went over and squeezed Quacksie.

"What wuzzat?" Daryl giggled just as Angie came into the room, swiping at Darlene's face with a wash cloth. She smiled. "He's really smart, isn't he?" she said.

7

Three Mothers

A few days later Angie called and asked me to go with her to visit Kathy.

"I don't know, Ange," I said evasively. "I don't think we have anything in common anymore." I'd meant to say that I didn't have anything in common with Kathy, but it came out as if I meant both of them.

"What do you mean?" Angie was understandably insulted. "We're all mothers. And we've been friends for years. Isn't that enough?"

I didn't tell her about the time I'd had Kathy and her husband George over for dinner. Daryl had been particularly trying that day, throwing up and crying, while I attempted to cook a gourmet meal. Kathy, pregnant with twins at the time, expressed wonder at my perfect table setting, my elegant stuffed shrimp, the homemade dessert. Daryl was fussing, and I rocked him as I talked to her. "It wouldn't have been hard," I blurted out unthinkingly, "if it wasn't for *him*."

Kathy's jaw dropped. "Well, isn't that just too bad," she said in a scolding voice.

"Come on, we'll have fun," Angie insisted. "She wants to see you. And you need to get out of the house."

Since marriage and motherhood, Kathy had gained a good fifty pounds. She greeted us in a flowered housedress. "It's about time!" she boomed, taking Darlene from Angie's arms. She held her up and studied her little face. "And who are you, pretty girl? You can't possibly belong to this old woman, you're too gorgeous."

Angie laughed good-naturedly, while I inwardly noted that Kathy had never held Daryl.

Kathy's year-old twin girls sat on a blanket on the living room carpet. After much fussing and gushing over the babies, we spent a good half-hour setting them up with an assortment of toys. Kathy turned the television to cartoons. Hesitantly I placed Daryl on the floor in his infant seat; I felt uneasy leaving him in such a vulnerable position with the other babies, but admonished myself to relax and let him be a "normal" child. This is the first time I remember feeling utterly confused about how to treat Daryl, torn between wanting to keep him safe and wanting to treat him "normal." It was certainly not the last.

We retired to the kitchen to begin an endless stream of coffee and cigarettes. Kathy and Angie, who'd both been Navy wives until recently, compared notes—mostly a litany of complaints.

"The air in Japan was disgusting," Angie said. "When I hung my sheets to dry they ended up black from all the soot. I had to hang them in the bathroom. You wouldn't believe what a filthy country it is—men pissed in the streets like it was a public toilet."

"I hated San Diego," Kathy chimed in. "I was so happy to come home. I can't imagine being in a foreign country, you poor kid."

"Did you see the Pacific Ocean?" I asked her.

Kathy shrugged. "You've seen one ocean, you've seen them all."

Leave it to fate, I thought, to let these two ingrates travel the world while I'd remained stuck on Long Island.

"Those Navy doctors," Angie said, forcefully stubbing out a cigarette. "I swear they didn't know the first thing about delivering babies. I was in labor for twenty-six hours with no painkillers or anything."

"You poor thing," Kathy said in mock sympathy. "Try having twins Try a C-section."

I wanted to speak, to say something about my particular horrific birth experience, but the words stuck like glue in my throat. If Kathy had no sympathy for Angie, why would she have any to spare for me? Also, it felt too much like we were competing for who'd had the hardest time—a competition that I felt, by almost any standard, I had won hands down without saying a word.

Suddenly a loud crash sounded from the living room, followed by a scream and a wail. I was on my feet instantly, Angie right behind, Kathy lumbering after us. Daryl lay on his side strapped into the plastic seat. His forehead bore a red mark, obviously from some thrown object. Darlene stood in front of him, looking puzzled. One of the twins was whimpering; the other watched in wide-eyed curiosity.

My heart dropped to my stomach, and my stomach felt like it had fallen out through my vagina. Quickly I righted the infant seat, undid the straps and took Daryl out. In a few seconds he stopped crying; but for the fading mark on his forehead, he seemed unharmed.

Angie swooped down on Darlene, slapping her on the hand. "Bad girl." Darlene let out a shriek that spiraled into wild sobbing.

"It's okay, Angie, he's fine," I assured her, devastated that she'd hit Darlene.

Kathy turned to the startled twins, frowning. "What are you two looking at?"

"She has to learn not to hit other kids," Angie insisted. "Come on, you're going down for a nap."

"Oh, leave her," Kathy said. "Here, we'll put the girls in the playpen." She dragged a folded playpen from the hall and Angie helped her set it up. The twins were plopped inside without much ado, but Darlene cried and pulled at the sides.

"No," Angie insisted. "You're staying in there now." Kathy distributed cookies, and soon everyone quieted down. I took Daryl into the kitchen, setting him in his seat on the floor, inwardly admonishing myself for having left him open to the attack.

Kathy looked at him warily. "Can something like that hurt his uh, his head?"

"The doctor says it's not that easy to damage the shunt."

"Is that what that scar is?" Angie asked.

"Yeah. It drains the fluid."

In silence we stirred sugar into fresh cups of coffee. I wondered what they were thinking, and hoped they wouldn't ask me more questions about Daryl's condition.

Finally Angie said, "It's a bitch, isn't it? I mean, nobody told us how hard this would be."

"You got that right," Kathy said.

"Yeah," I sighed, feeling connected to them at last.

"You hungry?" Kathy asked after another short silence.

"Yeah. What's for lunch?"

Kathy heaved herself out of her chair and opened a cabinet to reveal row upon row of small colored jars. "Strained carrots, rice pudding, beef, apricots...."

"God, I hate that shit!" I said.

"Then help me make tuna fish."

"That is so like you, Kathy," I complained. "You don't see me for six months and when I do come visit you I have to make my own lunch." My mood was lightening up; I was beginning to remember why I loved these two women.

Angie giggled. "Now," she said, tears forming in her eyes, "Now I feel like I'm finally home."

The day's activities wiped Daryl out; he actually slept through most of the night—but I couldn't. I lay beside Bob, thinking jealously about Darlene, and of Kathy's twins—cute healthy little girls. I wanted one. I wanted a daughter, a baby, a healthy baby. Though I hadn't given much previous thought to having more children, I was suddenly seized with an overwhelming urge to hold an infant in my arms again.

Bob stirred in his sleep and I nestled my body up against him. Reaching down, I took his penis in my hand, slowly bringing it to an erection. Half asleep, he rolled over and lazily entered me.

Nine months later when I held Stacy in my arms and received visitors, I understood exactly why she'd been brought into this world: my beautiful little girl was perfectly normal.

Stacy was, besides normal, a very easy baby to care for. She operated on a precise inner clock that kept her asleep for five-hour intervals between feedings. After my trial by fire with Daryl, I felt like an old hand at motherhood—as the late great Dr. Spock said, every parent should have their second child first.

Stacy's birth had satisfied a lifelong itch; for as long as I could remember, I'd been obsessed with wanting a daughter. But now she was here, the itch had been scratched, it was enough. I felt a strange detachment, as though I need do nothing more for this girlchild. Daryl's condition had stabilized, and he was finally walking.

I was finished with baby-making. I was ready to move on.

8

Consequences

A photograph. Daryl and Stacy stand in front of our eight-room sprawling ranch house, holding hands. She wears a pink dress and tiny beribboned pigtails; he is dressed in a brown tweed suit and new horn-rimmed glasses; he is clutching an oversized briefcase. It is Daryl's first day of school.

All summer I'd been preparing him for the event, painting a rosy picture of the children he would meet, the games he would play, the things he would learn. Thus he was eager to embark on this adventure, and happily waved goodbye from the yellow bus.

Three hours later he emerged from the same bus, pushing at his glasses, wearing a dazed expression.

"Well?" I asked eagerly. "How was it?"

He looked at me for just an instant, a look of accusation that sent a chill down my spine, before his eyes glazed over. "Fine."

"Did you like it? Did you make any friends? What did you do?"

"It was fine," he repeated expressionlessly. I had the sinking sensation that he no longer trusted me.

A few days later I received a note from the school principal to the effect that Daryl could not use the playground equipment without a consenting note from his physician. Bob and I had, when we'd registered Daryl for school, informed them of his condition, primarily so they would know what to do in an emergency. We naively believed this was sufficient. We'd never dreamt that they'd treat Daryl any differently from the other children. He used the swing and slide we'd set up in the backyard without any problem.

55

I asked Daryl if he'd been using the swings and slides.

"No," he answered coolly, "I like to sit and talk to the teacher."

Dr. Abrams sent the school his written permission, absolving them of responsibility in case of accident, and, after two weeks of sitting on the sidelines, Daryl was allowed to play with the other children.

Shortly thereafter I was summoned to a parent-teacher conference.

Sitting before Miss Raymond in the classroom, memories of my own school years came rushing back, and I felt exactly as I'd felt then: intimidated by authority. I sat mutely while Miss Raymond took some papers out of a folder.

"You see how he scribbles all over the page?" she said, frowning. "I was wondering if perhaps his medical condition affects his ability to color within the lines."

"Well, they told us he does have some perceptual problems," I said. "But I've seen him do better than that in his coloring books. Maybe he just likes to scribble—that can be fun too."

Miss Raymond removed her glasses and pensively chewed on the tip. "Maybe it's fun," she said in measured tones, "but I have asked him time and again to color in the lines. I wonder—how do you discipline Daryl?"

"Discipline?" I swear to God, I had never had occasion to consider the matter.

"Yes. What are the consequences of Daryl's actions?"

I simply stared at her.

"You see, Mrs. H., the kindergarten class isn't just a playroom, as most people seem to think. This is where we lay the foundation for all of Daryl's education. It's very important that he learn to follow orders."

This child, who had twice faced death in the form of surgical procedures, who had seen more varieties of human suffering than most adults, was nonetheless bright, cheerful, and unusually articulate. Everyone who knew him felt he was destined for something special. This child enters school. He is told when to sit, when to stand, when to talk and when to be quiet. For half an hour each day, when the other children are released at last to play, he is told he cannot go on the swings.

He refuses to color in the lines.

I went home, feeling positively numb. Here I'd been convinced I'd given birth to a genius who would be welcomed as such by the American school system. Sure, he had a physical problem, but intellectually he was way ahead of most kids I knew. I had anticipated an entirely different scenario for my first parent/teacher conference. Now I wondered what I had done to produce such a misfit.

Later that day I took the kids to visit my mother. After Daryl had painted her long talon-like fingernails, interestingly enough without a smear, and was off playing with his sister, I told my mother, who shared my belief in Daryl's superior intelligence, about the conference. She was partly amused, partly astounded. "They are insane," she declared with a laugh.

◆   ◆   ◆

While Daryl was coping with kindergarten, Dr. Abrams was, unbeknownst to us, cracking under the strain of his profession.

He was one of the leading pediatric neurosurgeons in the country, whose exclusive focus had become the treatment of hydrocephalus. He had performed the same shunt operation thousands of times, and was involved in research to find new treatments. Often during Daryl's routine checkups he would tell us anecdotes about his other patients. On one visit, he suddenly leaned back in his swivel chair, pointed out the window at the grimy brick buildings, and demanded, "Is this any way to live? I ask you, is this what we were born to do?"

"Maybe you need a vacation," Bob offered.

"Vacation! Hah! Who'd take care of my kids?"

"Yeah," Bob conceded, "I guess you're right."

"You're damn straight I'm right. How would you like it if Daryl's shunt malfunctioned while I was off on a Caribbean cruise?"

Bob and I exchanged an uneasy look. Oblivious to our discomfort, the doctor continued. "You know what happened to one of my kids last week? She fell down the stairs and cracked her shunt."

I uttered a small 'oh.' Dr. Abrams shot me a glare. "You think that's bad, do you? Well, that isn't even the half of it. I believe she was thrown down those stairs. I mean, did you ever hear of a five-month old being left to crawl around at the top of the stairs? And the kid can't even crawl, fachrissakes."

We listened in shocked silence.

"If you could have seen that woman's face..." He removed his glasses and wearily rubbed his eyes. "A dreadful business."

Suddenly he blinked and shook his head, as if just becoming aware of our presence. "Daryl's doing fine," he said. "You can go now."

Slowly we rose. "Go, go," Dr. Abrams muttered. "Go home and take care of your son."

"That was weird," I said to Bob as we drove home. "What do you think is going on with Dr. Abrams?"

"I guess it's getting to him. All these kids, all these operations."

I shivered. "What will we do if he cracks up?"

"We'll find another doctor."

"Yeah? Remember the quack?"

Bob shrugged. "We'll worry about it when the time comes."

A few weeks later we received a letter from a Dr. Fred Epstein informing us that he was assuming Dr. Abrams' practice.

"How can they just switch doctors on us?" Bob raved. He did some investigating through a doctor friend, and learned that Dr. Abrams had indeed had a nervous breakdown.

In the long run, this actually turned out to be a blessing. Dr. Epstein's bedside manner was a vast improvement over that of Dr. Abrams. On our first visit, as we sat in the waiting room, he emerged from his office, his arm around a mother's shoulder.

"Don't worry," he was telling her. "You're doing a great job. You're doing everything just right."

It was a small thing, an easy gesture. But no one, much less a doctor, had ever once said it to me; I instantly loved Daryl's new doctor, who was to become an internationally acclaimed neurosurgeon. Besides being an excellent surgeon, Dr. Epstein was charming, empathetic, and easy to talk to. I 'm probably not the only mother of one of his patients who developed a crush on him; after my divorce, I entertained fantasies of marrying the handsome Dr. Epstein, thereby attaining a unique kind of security for my son.

9

Becoming Conscious

Oh yes, there was a divorce—when Daryl was five and Stacy three.

In *A Difference in the Family*, an otherwise outstanding book on families of children with disabilities, author Helen Featherstone makes virtually no mention of broken marriages or their effect on disabled children; she makes the astonishing claim that "most marriages survive" having a child with a disability. At the time I read this, I wondered if perhaps the burden of caring for a special needs child tends to hold couples together, that perhaps my marriage was an aberration.

But *A Difference in the Family* was written two decades ago; a recently published book, *Special Kids Need Special Parents*, by Judith Loseff Lavin, cites a fifty percent divorce rate in families where a child has or develops problems. Did the divorce rate take a giant leap in the past twenty years? Did parents of kids with disabilities decide *en masse* to throw in the towel? No: what happened is that, as in other areas of public discourse on the subject of disability, we've become more knowledgeable, as well as more honest.

It's difficult for me to know for sure how much Daryl's disability contributed to my marital problems, but the more I read and learn, the more significant it appears to have been. I think we probably would not have lasted anyway: from the outset we had several strikes against us. We were very young; we hardly knew each other; we differed in philosophical outlook and basic values; ours had been a "shotgun wedding." Not that our marriage was completely awful: during the first few months we did begin to know and adjust to one another, and even shared moments of genuine love. But our level of communication was in the embryonic stage, and when we were thrust so suddenly into a difficult situation, there just wasn't any structure in place to enable us to communicate about it. We were each overwhelmed in our own way, groping to deal with what was happening. We each harbored distrust and resentment, silently blaming each other and ourselves.

But it was that way about everything, not just about Daryl. That we were burdened with extra responsibility put an added strain on our relationship, but I have little doubt that we would have divorced regardless. We were a statistic of an era: the factors that led to the dissolution of our marriage were the same ones that eroded the marriages of so many of our peers, and have been well documented by sociologists. Daryl's condition was a factor, but not the determining one.

We took six months to finally separate, during which time we alternately sought counseling, phoned our respective lawyers, moved in and out of the house, and generally tortured each other. During this period I read Betty Friedan's *The Feminine Mystique* and informed Bob that the only way he could possibly save our marriage was to read it too. He didn't, and I joined one of the women's consciousness-raising groups that were popping up in all corners of the country.

Most of the women in my CR group were wives of professors from the nearby university; all were mothers. The first few sessions opened vast areas of insight and feeling within me; in our discussions of our roles as housewives, our upbringing as females, our schooling, our husbands, fathers and mothers, there was always a common thread holding us together. For all of us, a lifetime's isolation was eased by the understanding of shared experience.

Despite our common female experience, though, I still felt a difference here; the others were for the most part older than I was, were college educated, and had married men who were on some level attempting to change. I, on the other hand, was a working class child bride whose higher education consisted of a year at a community college and whose husband called me "wacko" for joining such a group.

Our discussions were generated by a list that came from the National Organization for Women; each woman would first relate her experience, uninterrupted, before anyone could speak a second time. At our seventh or eighth meeting we addressed the issue of childbirth and motherhood.

The first speaker described the birth of her first child, who had been delivered by Lamaze. I listened, thinking the story not so different from those told at any coffee klatch; although some of the details differed, the essence remained— women relished the chance to relate perhaps the most intense experience of their lives. So I thought, listening with a certain degree of detachment, momentarily forgetting that eventually it would be my turn to speak.

The topic generated so much excitement that our usual format disintegrated; everyone began speaking at once. I became increasingly anxious as memories of Daryl's birth and infancy flooded over me while I listened to their stories—some shot through with humor, some of difficult labors, but all ultimately exhilarating.

"Those first few weeks I couldn't relate to anything else—all I wanted was to be with my baby."

Those early days in the hospital, with Daryl undergoing tests and surgery.

"When I saw her I couldn't believe I'd created such a perfect creature."

Yes, I had felt that way with Daryl—for perhaps sixteen hours. With Stacy, I hadn't believed it for months.

"I was so scared I'd do something wrong, that I'd hurt her."

Daryl's first doctor telling me to push on his fontanel, and me thinking it would hurt him.

"Did yours ever have colic? God, it drove me insane."

Try projectile vomiting.

"I couldn't wait for her to start crawling, but once she did I never got a moment's rest."

Daryl was eighteen months old before he crawled.

"The first time he scratched himself I cried as if it was my own flesh."

His scalp injected with dye, slit open, re-stitched.

"Getting up every four hours—that was the worst."

Walking the floor all night, rocking him in the carriage.

"The pediatrician's office! Two hours in a waiting room with nine frantic mothers and fourteen snotty-nosed kids."

The neurosurgeon's office: two hours with children in wheelchairs, babies with bandaged heads. The therapists' office: thalidomide babies, Downs Syndrome, spina bifida. The growth specialist. The hospital wards. The waiting rooms. The waiting.

"And then he'd just tell you something simple like add applesauce to her diet."

And then he'd just tell you something simple like push on his fontanel have him sleep sitting up measure his head every day call me if it grows.

How could I fling into the center of this bubbly congregation my bitter fury? I made a feeble attempt: catching Marcia's eyes I murmured, "My son was born with a birth defect." (By now I knew that no one had ever heard of hydrocephalus.) "He had to have operations."

A look of—what? Chagrin? Revulsion? Fear? crossed her face, and she turned away, eager to rejoin the laughter and happy chatter of the others.

A literal chill crept over my neck: it was the chill of isolation. Almost immediately I sought to alleviate it, wrapping myself in a protective cloak of smug superiority: so, this was what the Women's Liberation Movement had to offer. For all their intellectual finesse, their knowledge of politics and culture, they were hopelessly naive. This hen party was no road to enlightenment, and these pretentious women were deluded snobs for thinking it was. Ultimately, these "consciousness-raising" sessions were no more enlightening than my coffee klatches with Angie and Kathy.

The next morning I lay in bed listening to the sounds of Sesame Street while Daryl and Stacy ate dry cereal in the playroom. Bob had moved into a motel a few days earlier, and there was a pleasant sense of mild disorganization in the house, unsettling and liberating at the same time. I no longer felt compelled to jump out of bed, feed the kids a hot breakfast and get to work scrubbing my house. My previous schedule, seemingly self-imposed, had disintegrated: once my husband was gone, a little mildew on the bathroom tiles seemed insignificant. I was actually enjoying my house for the first time; no longer was it an entity to be pampered, but a space to live in. I allowed myself the luxury of lying in bed, thinking about the previous night's meeting.

I was angry with the women's group: how could they have allowed our regular format to break down and leave me no space to tell my story? I berated myself for not speaking up, but then I remembered Marcia's face, her inability to hear what I was saying. It was almost as if they'd formed a conspiracy of silence against anything unpleasant—odd, when you considered that our other sessions were usually bitter tirades against husbands, society, "the patriarchy."

I got out of bed, put on a robe, and went to the playroom. Daryl and Stacy sat in front of the TV amid a sea of cereal crumbs and several serving-size boxes.

"Can we go outside?" Daryl asked. It was Spring, and they had just reached the age where they played with the other children on the block; there was a group of nine altogether, ranging in age from three to seven, who roamed from one backyard and kitchen to another all day.

I helped them dress, sent them out with my usual admonitions about traffic—practically non-existent on our street—and made myself a cup of coffee. This new street life of theirs, combined with Bob's absence, afforded me more solitude than I'd had in six years.

As I continued to mull over the meeting, my thoughts wandered to the circumstances that had created my anger in the first place: Daryl's birth and infancy. A whole block of time seemed, in my memory, to be shrouded in white: white walls, white sheets, white coats—the medical establishment. The awful obstetrician who'd intimidated me into bad eating habits, shot me full of drugs and then "reassured" me that I could have more kids. The nurses who'd pumped me full of pills. All the cold-hearted specialists who'd mindlessly pushed on my little baby's vulnerable soft spot with their big-knuckled hairy fingers. The incompetent neurosurgeon, who'd kept Daryl as a patient long after he could do anything for him. Dr. Abrams, who'd treated Daryl as an interesting specimen and ultimately abandoned us. Dozens of nurses, therapists and technicians, none of whom had ever given me one word of empathy or encouragement.

Alone in my sunny kitchen, I was seized with a fury so strong it was frightening: I had never learned to express anger, which I equated with violence. Shakily I took out a pen and notebook and began composing irrational letters to various doctors, my handwriting nearly illegible. I wrote page after page until, realizing the futility of my undertaking, I ripped them all up.

"What a waste of time," I sobbed into the empty kitchen.

The doorbell rang. I composed myself and answered: Stacy had to use the bathroom, and one of the older children had escorted her home. After the bathroom there was the mandatory cookie distribution, and they went back to their street friends.

I resumed my vigil at the table, reviewing every wrong that had been perpetrated against me. In hindsight, I now realize that the consciousness-raising group came at the precise moment that I was ripe for confronting long-buried feelings. My separation from Bob had put me into an introspective frame of mind: by taking the risk of divorce I had allowed myself to take other risks as well, including looking more honestly at my life. Also, since Daryl hadn't required extensive medical attention in years, I was far enough removed from the worst of the situation to be able to put some of it into perspective.

Not that I had any notion then of what I was doing: I did not. My experience with psychotherapy was limited to a couple of marriage counseling sessions, the CR group, and a few pop psych paperbacks. I had no maps or charts for the journey I embarked upon by myself in my kitchen that morning.

I called my sister, and babbled out my rage at the medical establishment. "How could they have treated us so coldly?" I ranted. "How could I have passively gone along with them?"

"Hey," she said soothingly, "it's good you were that way. You never would have gotten through it if you'd been like this."

"What are you telling me?" I screamed. "Are you telling me it was better when I kept my mouth shut?"

"Look, you were terrific for Daryl—we all thought so. Don't put yourself down about it now."

"Who said I was putting myself down?" I felt enormously frustrated: I was not getting through. Even when I clearly expressed my feelings, I still wasn't understood. "I'm not putting myself down! Just the opposite—I'm pissed off!"

"What good will that do?"

Furious, I hung up on her. Now my rage found a new target: my family. My family, who kept a lid on their emotions and wanted me to do likewise. My family, who, I was beginning to see, lived in denial. Why hadn't they helped more? Where were they during those long hospital nights when I'd roamed the halls and waiting rooms by myself?

I remembered those lonely days and nights in the hospital. Where were my supposed best friends: Angie and Kathy had run off to exotic lands, leaving me to cope all alone. Angie should have come home when she got the news: it was the *least* she could have done.

Daryl and Stacy came in for lunch; distractedly I made PB&J sandwiches. When they asked for cookies I exploded—possibly the first time I'd ever yelled at them without any real provocation.

"Get out! Get outside! I can't take it!" I shoved a box of cookies into Daryl's hand and they retreated with frightened faces.

Still in my nightgown, I opened a bottle of wine. It was a short step from being mad at Angie to being mad at Bob. When I thought about his behavior all these years, anger threatened to engulf me. I downed several glasses of wine.

Bob had offered little practical help with Daryl; worse, he'd sabotaged my efforts at motherhood by hovering over me, questioning every little detail, undermining my confidence. And then there was his betrayal, his concealment of Daryl's condition, a deception that had seriously eroded my sense of reality, destroyed my trust in him, and later on made me neurotic about Stacy. I gripped the wineglass, hatred towards my husband firing up every cell in my bloodstream. Had Bob walked in right then, I would have wrung his neck.

The doorbell rang: Stacy needing the bathroom again. Really, I thought, ushering her out when she was done, this child was carrying toilet training to an extreme.

I continued guzzling wine, planning what I would say to Bob the next time I saw him. I started writing him a letter but was once more interrupted by the doorbell: Stacy yet again. She cast furtive glances at my exasperated face, did her business, and departed. A few minutes later the bell rang again.

"Jesus Christ," I hollered, storming to the door, "I'm gonna have your fucking kidneys X-rayed."

A young woman with a shiny scrubbed face stood on the other side of the screen door holding a copy of *Awake*. Stacy stood by her side sucking her thumb, her eyes wide with interest.

"I, uh, I came to bring you the word of the Lord."

"Oh," I said sheepishly, "I'm sorry. It's just that she's been in and out all day."

"May I come in?"

Now, I had never in my life admitted a Jehovah's Witness into my home, but in my shame and confusion I began to open the door.

"No," I said, catching myself, "I'll just take one of your pamphlets.

Visibly relieved, the woman tottered down the driveway on her high heels. As I watched her retreating back, I began to chortle maniacally.

"Serves her right," I said, slapping my thigh in drunken glee. "Those damn religious nuts shouldn't be invading my privacy."

Stacy looked at me queerly, and in her confused little face I saw myself, her previously solid mother, now a disheveled mess in nightgown and bathrobe, drunk at three in the afternoon.

"Oh baby," I said, lifting her up. "I'm sorry. Did Mommy scare you?" I took her inside, sat on the rocker with her, and read stories. After awhile she seemed reassured and went back outside to play.

I switched from wine to coffee, but continued to seethe with anger for the rest of the afternoon. Somehow I managed to maintain a reasonably calm exterior for the children. I went through the motions of dinner and bedtime preparations in silence while they, confused by a side of me they'd never seen, were unusually subdued. Instead of reading them a story, I suggested that Daryl read to Stacy, and he complied, showing her pictures and verbalizing the few words he remembered or recognized.

I've read similar accounts by women of my generation, documenting the changes they went through as they became more self-aware, changes that led to the dissolution of their marriages. At the time, we told ourselves that an unhealthy marriage was worse for children than a healthy divorce, a philosophy vigorously reinforced by the "experts" of the day.

But there is no such thing as a healthy divorce when children are part of the equation. Years later, new studies would prove that divorce is almost always traumatic and destructive for children. I didn't have to read these studies, however, to know the truth early on—and I suspect that many of my peers secretly knew it as well: we could not help but notice the way our breakups played out for our kids. The effects on them were emotionally and financially devastating—and make no mistake about it, the financial loss dramatically affected the quality of their lives far into the future.

I am not saying that men and women should stay in bad relationships for the sake of the kids. But I am saying that in those days our
definition of a "bad relationship" was hopelessly unrealistic. Far too
many of us threw in the towel with the blink of an eye; in a different
social climate, many might have stuck it out and made the marriages
work.

Nor am I saying that I should have stayed with Bob, or that I regret
not having done so; indeed, in subsequent years his increasingly cruel
behavior showed me that I'd been right to leave him. But in the interests of full disclosure I must face the fact that divorce was damag-
ing—perhaps even more so than staying together would have been—to
both of my children.

Perhaps if I had used the divorce to grow in a more positive direction, becoming more rational and grounded, then I might be able to
say that the divorce was of some benefit to them. But my journey of
self-discovery came at their expense. I did not become more rational or
grounded for another fifteen years, by which time they were nearly
grown. The day that I spent in my kitchen crying and writing letters to
doctors, shouting at my sister and frightening my daughter with
drunken behavior was just the first of many such episodes. Over the
next two decades I continued my quest for self-knowledge, as I saw it,
sometimes fortified by alcohol, sometimes with other mind-altering
substances. To put it mildly, I was a moody and erratic mother.

After they were in bed I sat on the sofa while the room darkened.
Twilight had become a melancholy time for me. I was learning to face
long lonely nights, fortified by my books and, increasingly, alcohol.

A car pulled up in the driveway; nervously I ran to the window and
saw Bob's newly acquired Cadillac. I shuddered; two nights ago he'd
barged in with threats to commit me to a mental institution; the night
before he'd arrived with roses, begging for another chance. But tonight
he simply came to the door and said he wanted to pick up some
clothes.

I remained in the living room while he visited with the children, my anger rekindled by his presence. I heard him enter the bedroom and open the closet. Downing another glass of wine, I marched inside where he stood selecting ties from the rack.

"I have to talk to you."

He looked me up and down with undisguised contempt.

I closed the bedroom door. "I've been thinking all day about Daryl, about how it was—the doctors, my family, you and me."

His face softened slightly; he regarded me with interest.

"Everyone was awful," I said, bursting into tears. "I can't believe how bad it all was, how no one ever helped, how alone I felt."

"Oh, babe," he said, relief visible on his face, "I understand." He opened his arms and moved to embrace me.

Forcefully I pushed him away. "Oh no you don't, you bastard. It's too late."

Feeling more pain than anger now, I ran into the spare bedroom and locked the door. Leaning up against it, I sobbed, clutching my aching stomach. Beneath the anger, or mixed in with it, was a level of emotional pain that I had never even imagined. I had opened a vast, gaping wound and had no idea how to begin to heal it. One thing I did know for sure, however: I would not allow myself to be vulnerable to Bob. I did not want him to see my pain, lest he use it as a way of hooking me back into the marriage. His betrayal had been too devastating to forgive.

I remained behind the locked door, fearful that Bob might retaliate with violence. I heard him go in to the children, and wondered if he'd whisk them away, accusing me of negligence. But no, he was speaking softly, kissing them goodnight, ushering Stacy into her room. Maybe he was planning to knock down the door and beat me up after they were asleep—he had hit me once or twice before. I listened with relief as he quietly left the house, then crept to the window to watch him. His shoulders slumped in resignation; carrying an overnight bag, he slowly got into the car, casting a final worried look at the house.

Suddenly the obvious hit me: he had been deeply moved by my outburst. He had been hurting too.

10

The Biggest Mistake

We sold our house and I, naively thinking I could still play out some of my adolescent fantasies—primarily, living like a bohemian artist—moved into a two-room apartment on the Upper West Side of Manhattan. The kids shared the only bedroom; I slept on the sofa. I was thrilled to be in New York, to be working in the women's movement, to be "free." I sampled liberally from the counterculture—I threw out my bra, wrapped tie-dyed headbands around my long flowing hair and wore faded jeans or long cotton "Granny dresses." I smoked pot daily. I hooked up with a long-haired guitar-playing chess master who lived from one crash pad to another, and who promptly moved in to share my sofa.

The kids were less than enthusiastic about our drastically altered lifestyle—but I paid little attention to their dissatisfactions. During the next few years I restlessly dragged them on my quest for adventure—from the city to the artists' colony of Woodstock, then from a small house to a commune to a rustic, electricity-less cabin in the woods. A series of men paraded through my life; my friends were all colorful characters involved in the arts or left-wing politics. In the spirit of the times I opened my home to anyone who needed shelter, more than once helping single mothers or battered wives relocate to Woodstock from the city, their children bunking with mine. A pot of soup or chili tofu was always simmering on my stove.

I was oblivious to any problems the kids had adjusting from one school to another, each with a progressively more radical philosophy of education. Now I regret giving them no choice but to come along on my journey of self-discovery. But at the time, I convinced myself they were benefiting from exposure to so many unusual places and people. Maybe they did; they learned a lot of offbeat skills, including origami, guitar frets and the hidden meaning of Bob Dylan lyrics. But these things did not compensate for the chaos and insecurity of their daily lives.

I fervidly believed in the hippie dream; the Age of Aquarius was upon us. We free spirits and feminists were ushering in an entirely new society, and partly through my efforts, my children would inherit a better world.

Okay, I was young and inexperienced. I'd never had an opportunity to explore who I was or how I wanted to live. That's the reason I neglected the needs of my children—there are always reasons. But there are no excuses. Now when I tell people I was a "bad mother" they inevitably try to reassure me, frequently with the stock phrase "You did the best you could." This leaves me as cold as that old standby, "I don't know how you do it."

Recently I was visiting Angie on Long Island, and Kathy and her husband came over. George and Jimmy retired to the den, leaving us women in the kitchen for one of our gabfests; although Angie and I talk regularly on the phone, it'd been several years since I'd spoken to Kathy. Nothing else in the world is like being with old friends who know each other's history. Our talk ranged forward and back, up and down, spanning decades, encompassing generations. I don't remember how it came up, but I was telling them how much I regret the things I did and did not do for Daryl as a child with a disability. Angie, as she usually does when I get on this track, began muttering phrases like "you were young," and "you were in denial." I kept insisting that I could have done so much more to help Daryl overcome his issues; I told her that I've met people who've done better than I did with disabled kids. Still, she refuted me, thinking she was being kind—or maybe thinking that is what I wanted to hear. I was near tears, frustrated by my inability to make her hear what I was saying. Finally Kathy broke in.

"Ange, can't you see? She's trying to say that some kids with disabilities do better because their parents did things differently. That she could have done more for him."

Such a statement might have generated paranoia—it could be taken as criticism, as something Kathy might have felt all along about me. But when I looked at her face, I saw no judgment. I saw no triumph, no "I-told-you-so." She was merely acknowledging what I was saying. She trusted that I knew what I was talking about.

It was a huge relief. It felt so much better to be acknowledged, believed, *trusted*, rather than made to "feel better" with stock phrases and white lies. Because the bald truth is,

I could have and should have done better. I don't want clichéd reassurances now; I want a realistic assessment of my behavior. I want to make up for my mistakes, and over the years I've made some progress. I've had to get over my guilt, which is useless, even crippling. I want to stop feeling guilty, yes, but to exonerate myself entirely, no. You can only make amends when you admit there's something to make amends for in the first place.

Fortunately, during this time Daryl didn't have any overt problems related to hydrocephalus. His shunt was working, he was developing normally; things were going so well that he only saw the neurosurgeon for an annual checkup.

About three years after the divorce, the kids went to visit Bob during Easter vacation. After a week he called and asked if they could stay a few extra days. He didn't have to ask: by this time I welcomed his visits with the kids as vacations. I was doing drugs—the ubiquitous marijuana and occasionally hallucinogenics—and I cherished solitude as a time to explore my psyche.

The days went by, and then Bob called again. The kids were having a blast, could they stay another few days. Sure, I said. I lit a joint and got back under the headphones.

This was the longest period of time I had ever spent alone in my entire life. I wrote in my journal, practiced yoga, listened to music, went for long walks in the woods. I began to imagine what it would be like to live alone all the time—not to have to get up and fix breakfast, take the kids to school, cook meals, be on call twenty-four/seven. I fantasized going to Europe, enrolling in college, writing a book or two. The more I thought about it, the more enticing the prospect became. I saw my life suddenly opening like a blank book: I could do anything, anything at all. It was a little bit scary, actually—but it was far more exciting.

I set about convincing myself of the rightness of letting the kids live with their father. This process is called rationalization, but at the time I thought it was clear thinking. Bob had remarried and could give them a proper family life; he had money and could give them everything they needed; men, as the women's movement proclaimed, were just as capable of raising children as were women; a mother's biology did not have to be her destiny. So thorough a job I did that I came to see my action as virtuous: I would be doing what was best for my children.

When they returned home, I wasted no time. I took Daryl aside and asked him how he felt about going to live with his father full time. Fresh from a successful visit, he liked the idea. I asked Stacy; she became confused and didn't answer me. I ignored her.

Thus it was decided. I called Bob and we arranged for a meeting where we ironed out the details. He was concerned I would change my mind and "bounce them around like ping pong balls." I dismissed his fears, the possibility of wanting the kids back the furthest thing from my mind. I wanted "freedom" so badly I could taste it. Nothing was going to get in my way. I refused to let anyone tell me to think more about it; a few friends tried, and were quickly silenced by my defensive rationalizations. In fact, I'd become so convinced I was doing the right thing that I managed to convince some of them as well. Later, when I realized my mistake, I wished that one of them had been more insistent—but I can hardly blame them, given my refusal to listen to any-one.

There is one person who I can and do blame—my therapist, who fully supported my decision. His view was a kind of knee-jerk therapy-centered one, based on the theory that the client's needs are para-mount, and that selfishness is a virtue. In the interests of my self-devel-opment, he thought that I was taking an important, brave and positive step by giving up my kids to Bob. He added to the self-justifications I'd created, finding new and loftier reasons for my decision. Not once did he inquire about what life would be like for my kids with Bob and Chris. He knew how I felt about their lifestyle and values, yet he never questioned my decision to let my children go live that lifestyle and be influenced by those values. Nor did he probe very deeply into what kind of effect this would all have on me, never postulated that I would inevitably feel guilty, or even that I might miss the kids. He never pointed out that I was giving up my maternal power, that I'd lose con-trol over their lives. Not once did he simply ask, "Are you sure you want to do this?"

I don't think that therapists are gods, or all-knowing wise men and women—far from it. But I do believe it's their job to guide clients into examining the ramifications of our actions. In this my therapist utterly failed me.

Years later, after the kids came back to live with me, I went to see him and confronted him. He 'fessed up: turned out that at the time he was treating me he had not seen his own son for almost ten years, since his wife had moved cross-country and he'd never pursued visitation rights. He now admitted that guilt about his own parental behavior had prevented him from offering me sound therapeutic guidance.

In any event, my children, six and eight years old, went back to Long Island to live with their father, his new wife, her daughter and the daughter they'd had together. I, who despised and rejected everything about the way they lived, sent my children to live that way.

It was the biggest mistake of my life.

11

Our Own Private Watergate

Two months after the children moved in with Bob, Daryl had his first seizure.

Although seizures are common in those who've had any kind of brain surgery, no doctor had ever warned us of this possibility. We had been told that the shunt could move out of place or malfunction, causing headaches, dizziness, and vomiting—but there had been no preparation for the moment when Daryl turned pale and incoherent and his body jerked violently in the grips of a grand mal seizure.

My immediate reaction to the news was, of course, self-blame. I was convinced that the seizure had been precipitated by the trauma of leaving his mother, changing his lifestyle, adapting to a stepmother. It seemed utterly logical—not a problem in seven years, he goes off to live with his father and has a seizure. (In fact, I have since learned that one of the factors contributing to the onset of seizures is stress—and certainly such a dramatic change in living situation is stressful for any child.)

At the time, I had only the vaguest notion of what a seizure was, and assumed that the shunt had malfunctioned. This did turn out to be the case in this instance; however, the scar tissue created by surgery and/or a foreign object in the head can lead to seizures, which consequently occur in many people with hydrocephalus.

It was late November; the first snow of the year was falling when I packed my bag and left for the hospital. During the two-hour drive, I was haunted by memories, guilt, self-pity and fear. Guilt: my abandonment of Daryl had caused the seizure. Self-pity: while other families sat cozy and warm around fireplaces, I was once more headed for a hospital. Fear: what exactly was happening to Daryl, and might he die? I marveled at how detached I'd been during his infancy; I could never be so emotionally removed again. Now I was so aware of every nuance of feeling that I was afraid I wouldn't be able to hold up.

Outside the hospital, striking employees were marching up and down, carrying signs and shouting. I was so distraught and confused I thought they were telling me, personally, that I couldn't enter the hospital. That is precisely what they were doing, though it was not quite as personal as I perceived it to be, and they glared accusingly as, for the first time in my life, I crossed a picket line.

I knew the route well: up the elevator to the ninth floor, turn to the right, through the swinging doors, down the hall to the nurses' station, every step weighted with memories, every odor carrying associations.

"I'd like to see Daryl H."

The nurse looked up from her chart. "Only parents are allowed to visit now."

"I'm his mother."

The nurse looked confused. "But his mother and father are already in there."

She might as well have pulled out a gun and shot me through the heart.

"That's his stepmother," I said, controlling my voice with great effort.

"Are you sure?"

"Do I have to show you my stretch marks?"

"I'm sorry. But they said they were his parents, and I just assumed...go on in, he's in the last room on the right."

As I entered the room I heard Daryl screaming, while a doctor and nurse tried to restrain him. Inwardly I shouted "Keep your hands off my baby!"

They were trying to put an IV into his arm; he was crying and flailing at them. Bob was attempting to calm him down, but Daryl didn't seem to hear, or even to be aware of his presence. Chris, Bob's wife, stood in a corner looking absolutely terrified. She glanced at me as I entered, her face registering frank hostility; I returned the look, furious at her for masquerading as the mother of my son.

It occurred to me that she'd never dreamed, when she'd agreed to raise Bob's children, what this would entail. I assumed that she hated me for dumping this mess into her lap, and begrudged me the freedom she imagined I had gained.

"Mommy's here," I said, edging towards the bed. He did not register my presence.

Somehow they managed to hook him up to the IV and sedate him. When he was finally asleep, we went into the lounge, and Bob told me what had happened.

They had been eating breakfast. One minute Daryl was talking to his stepsister, the next he was staring blindly into space, muttering disjointed, irrational phrases, his jaw moving up and down strangely. Alarmed, they had taken him to a local emergency room; apparently Bob had been dissatisfied with their response and decided to take Daryl straight into the city, to New York University and his doctors. There was a great deal of confusion in Bob's story; he hadn't had gas in his car and had been unable to obtain any; this was during a nation-wide gas shortage, when one could only purchase gas on specified days. So Bob, always one to enhance drama to the nth degree, contacted the police. A chaotic, siren-escorted ride had ensued, with Chris holding Daryl on her lap, where he'd begun to convulse.

"You didn't see it," Bob said repeatedly, shaking visibly. "You weren't there." His point seemed to be that I could not possibly understand the gravity of the situation—but underlying these statements was accusation, and I bristled defensively each time he said it.

Daryl had kept jerking, had thrown up, appeared to be nearly unconscious. Bob and Chris had no idea what to do; they'd thought he was dying.

Their obligation to me fulfilled by the telling of this story, they retreated to a corner to wait for Dr. Epstein.

Although a person having a grand mal seizure appears to be in severe danger, a seizure isn't a life-threatening situation—or so the doctors and medical texts blithely tell us. They say that so long as the person doesn't fall or hit any sharp objects, he or she will come to no harm, unless s/he passes from one seizure to another without regaining consciousness. But I have since heard of people choking to death for lack of oxygen, drowning in the shower, dying in their sleep during a seizure. I've been with Daryl for at least six of these episodes, and I have never gotten used to them. I have never really believed that Daryl will survive them.

I telephoned my parents, who had recently moved to the city, to say I needed to stay with them. My mother was due to leave for Florida the next morning, and my sister was about to go on vacation in Spain.

"Should I go?" my mother asked me.

With a wild desperation I wanted her to stay. "Go," I said automatically. "There's nothing you can do here."

It was the beginning of our worst and longest nightmare. Over the next four months, while the nation sat riveted to televised hearings of a criminal administration, we endured our own version of Watergate, and I couldn't tell you a thing about the real one. Daryl was in and out of the hospital three times and underwent as many operations, all against the backdrop of the holidays, excruciating tension and fights between Bob and me that once escalated to a physical skirmish, broken up by bystanders in the waiting room.

After a series of X-rays and tests, it was determined that the shunt had blocked and wasn't working properly, and that Daryl would need a surgical revision.

Throughout most of the first day Daryl was either being tested or sleeping. Bob roamed in and out of his room, checking to see if he was awake. On one of his sojourns he emerged to loudly announce, "Chris, he wants to see you."

Annoyed, I waited for her to finish visiting him; when she finally returned, she said he'd gone back to sleep.

Most of the hospital staff assumed that Chris was his mother; while I had reverted to using my maiden name, she shared his. Thus, in the intervals between their visits and Daryl's tests and naps, I invariably had to plead entry into his room, explaining our family structure. Hard as I tried to maintain civility, I could not ignore the fact that Bob and Chris were deliberately shutting me out.

When I had opted for daily freedom, I hadn't bargained for total abdication of my parental rights. Apparently Bob and Chris interpreted things differently, and though I was stunned by their attitude, my ever-present guilt kept me from confronting them.

The moments I shared with Daryl in his hospital room reassured me that our connection was still rock solid. What transpired in the halls and lounges took on the tinge of surrealistic drama, having little relation to the reality at Daryl's bedside.

He was frightened. He had learned to live with a shunt, X-rays and frequent medical examinations; now he was confronted with a highly unpredictable body. He rested in my arms, the fear within him palpable. I think that the time I spent holding him was the only time we both felt safe. We didn't need to speak much; he and Bob discussed the seizure and upcoming operation, but from his mother Daryl wanted non-verbal comfort. Likewise, I felt calm only when I was with him; it fortified me for what I faced outside his room.

At the end of the first day I returned to my parents' apartment, exhausted and drained. My mother had left for Florida, and my father wasn't home from work yet. Wearily I undressed and got into the shower. As the scalding water cascaded over me, the day's accumulated tension washed away, and I began to cry; a cleansing release soon escalated into uncontrollable sobs. My body shook and heaved; I threw up;

I couldn't stop. Frightened, I turned off the shower and got dressed, still sobbing.

In my family, emotional control has always been a virtue, tears evidence of weakness, if not outright insanity. I tried to get myself under control before my father arrived home.

The phone rang. "Hello," I whispered.

It was my great-aunt Ettie, a high-strung seventy-five year old woman who lived downstairs and who, I am happy to say, thrived on tragedy. She asked me how Daryl was.

"Fine," I answered automatically, and burst into fresh hysterics.

"I'm coming up," she said without hesitation.

"You'll have me locked up," I cried when she appeared. "I'm cracking up."

Aunt Ettie looked at me as if I had indeed gone mad. "Locked up? *Bubala,* it's natural for you to cry. Come, sit down and tell me all about it."

She led me to the kitchen table. "It's terrible to sit in a hospital all day when someone you love is sick. Didn't I sit there day after day while Grampa was dying? Didn't I spend months there with Uncle Mike? Who's going to blame you for crying?"

This was the first time anyone in my family had ever acknowledged, much less validated, my pain, and I was relieved beyond words. For nearly an hour my aunt and I tearfully exchanged hospital stories.

My father's key turned in the lock. Entering, he glanced up from a stack of mail and said a casual hello; his eyes roved the table, covered with soggy balled- up tissues, taking in the scene.

"So? How is he?"

It bothered me that he, like everyone at all times, never asked how I was. People politely enquired after the bare medical facts, never bothering to probe the layers underneath. And, of course, I felt guilty for wishing they'd ask about me as well as about Daryl.

"He needs an operation."

"So he'll have an operation." My father's tone was matter-of-fact, but his volume was almost a shout. As I continued to cry, he stared at me, baffled.

"Toby," said Aunt Ettie, "can't you see she's upset?"

My father turned abruptly and left the room.

"What is wrong with him?" Aunt Ettie murmured, patting my shoulder.

"He hates when I cry," I said, grabbing another tissue and trying to stifle myself.

My parents were children of the Depression, Jewish people just a generation removed from the Holocaust. They believed in putting the past behind, in hard work and little play, and absolutely no "self-indulgence," emotional or otherwise. But more particularly, they had never really accepted Daryl's disability. They never mentioned it, except out of necessity when he was in the hospital; otherwise they acted as if nothing was wrong. I'd even heard my mother tell friends and family about Daryl's birth without once mentioning hydrocephalus.

Ironically, my father had welcomed the opportunity to spend time alone with me, with my mother out of town. I suppose he thought we might become closer; my mother had often been a barrier between my father and me. Unfortunately, his idea of getting closer entailed lecturing rather than listening to me. In the end, I went to sleep vowing to keep my feelings to myself around my father—as I always had.

At six a.m. the hospital day is in full swing. Breakfast has been prepared and wheeled from room to room; only the most determined or comatose patient manages to sleep through the hubbub. Those awaiting surgery bear insult to injury, awake but unable to participate in the ceremony of breakfast.

Unlike his first operation eight years ago, Daryl understood why he couldn't eat; unlike his infant reaction, the lack of breakfast wasn't a significant deprivation. Not so for his mother, for whom the situation awakened old agonies.

"You can't eat," I explained apologetically, "because you might throw up under the anesthesia."

"I know," he replied nonchalantly. "Dr. Epstein told me."

He wasn't at all scared of the operation; he saw it as a corrective measure that would prevent more seizures, about which he was very concerned. I hadn't the heart to tell him that this was not necessarily so, that he would be put on anticonvulsant medication and that he might have more seizures in the future.

After he was given a tranquilizer and wheeled downstairs, Bob and Chris and I waved goodbye with false gaiety as the elevator doors closed. I sat down in the lounge, while they sat across the room. I was amused when they bent their heads together over a crossword puzzle, a hobby Bob had learned from me. I could no longer do puzzles, or read magazines; such diversions could not penetrate my thoughts and feelings. Within half an hour I was jumping out of my skin. Wanting to stretch my muscles and do some deep breathing, I made my way to the hospital's meditation room. Thankfully, there were no crosses or other religious icons in the dimly lit, thickly carpeted room, only an altar, fresh flowers and several unlit candles. I stretched out on the rug, and began my yoga practice. Suddenly I felt something sharp and painful pierce my scalp. I jumped up, stunned and terrified. I distinctly felt the cut of a knife slicing through my flesh, first in my scalp, then in my neck—precisely the points where Daryl's skin was being cut.

Mothers, they say, have problems separating from their children. We identify so closely with them, seeing them as an extension of ourselves, that we suffer every growing pain as if it was our own. In the most real sense, my child's pain was mine.

There was no way I was going to experience Daryl's surgery firsthand, so I abandoned yoga and the meditation room. In my purse was a small bottle of Valium reserved for emergencies; I took one. There is something to be said for emotional detachment after all.

The operation took nearly five hours. The Valium dulled my senses but did not entirely censor my thoughts. I worried that Daryl might be partially awake, feeling the pain of surgery as I had in the meditation room. Laced through all my thoughts was a sense of personal responsibility for his hardships. Although over the years I'd managed to partially absolve myself, conceding that it may not have been entirely my fault that my child had hydrocephalus, the guilt would never entirely disappear. How could it? How can a parent witness a child's suffering and not want to continually apologize? Rational arguments have no bearing; this is beyond the realm of rationality.

I imagined him dying under anesthesia. If it came to pass, I could see no future for me. I would never be able to face life without him, or the pity and consolation of others.

Across the room, Bob and Chris derived comfort from each other. Although I had felt as alone when I was married as I did now, Bob's physical presence had at least offered an illusion of support.

When I had left my marriage, other mothers had questioned me as to how I intended to raise my children by myself. I'd sloughed them off, confident of my ability to manage. Now I wondered what on earth I had been thinking.

12

There Must Be Some Way Out Of Here

Daryl went home for good—to live with Bob and Chris again—in February. The child who left the hospital after his first seizure, two shunt revisions and a scary infection was not the same child who'd entered it five months earlier. He was more uncertain, more aware of his disability, and frightened that his body might betray him without warning.

Not that I was keenly aware of Daryl's psychological condition. For the next three-plus years my kids continued to live with their father; I moved into Manhattan and took them every other weekend. I got an office job to pay the rent, joined a women's avant-garde theater group, and began writing my first novel. I loved living alone in Manhattan and I loved what I was doing. Creatively I was blossoming, and it was one of the most exciting periods of my life.

But it was also one of the most painful. I woke up every morning weighed down with guilt and sadness, emotions that I never quite learned how to distinguish from one another. I actually missed the kids fiercely, but in my confusion I attributed this to guilt—the guilt inevitably heaped upon mothers who play fast and loose with the traditional role. I fought against what I saw as irrational guilt, and rarely acknowledged the very rational desire to be with my kids. I started a support group for Mothers Without Custody; the women who joined worked hard to convince one another that what we were doing was fine, perhaps even heroic. Each week I presented my guilt to them and they dispelled it with theoretical arguments.

When I finally did come to the conclusion that it wasn't motherguilt but motherlove that was causing me so much pain, I was fully convinced that Bob wouldn't let me take them back without a fight. I imagined a custody battle, or even uglier scenarios involving kidnapping. I feared losing not only custody but also visitation rights. These fears were not completely off the wall; in those days men were starting to get custody of their children with greater frequency. Bob had financial resources; I did not. Bob had a "normal" family life; I did not. Bob knew how to manipulate the system; I did not. I had embarked on a love affair with a woman, and although neither the kids nor Bob knew about it, I was sure he'd find out—and "lesbianism" was and remains one of the most frequent reasons for a mother to lose custody.

Bob was actually having a difficult time with the kids, or at least with Daryl, but I did not grasp the full extent of it for quite some time. Daryl's perceptual problems were affecting his ability to learn—and schools had not yet become conscious about learning disabilities, nor tolerant of different learning styles. Bob interpreted Daryl's problems as pure laziness, and brutally punished him. To compound things, Chris had begun insisting that the children treat her as their true mother, and disapproved of or even punished them for expressing love towards me.

On the weekends when I had the kids, I could see that Daryl was becoming more and more withdrawn, less and less self-confident. Stacy was angry with me all the time, but didn't voice her reasons. After every weekend with them, I was despondent and confused. I should take them back, I told myself, and with this thought would come my terror of Bob. I have to admit that, just as strong as my terror was the desire to continue living by myself, exploring activities that I could not engage in as a full time mother. As the weekend visit receded in my memory, I'd gain some distance from these conflicting feelings—then the next visit rolled around and the cycle began all over again.

I was nearing a profound crisis point. The moment of truth arrived unexpectedly, in the form of another child's, and another mother's, crisis.

13

Someone Else's Child

March 20, 1976.

It is the evening before my thirtieth birthday. I am preparing to host a party for members of my theater group and other friends. Tonight my parents are taking me to see a Broadway show.

The telephone rings.

"Marce?"

I didn't immediately recognize the male voice.

"It's Jimmy." I was momentarily thrown; as far back as I could recall, Angie's husband had never called me. Without any preliminaries, he launched into a monologue, talking at death-defying speed, winding up with, "So here's what we're gonna do, we're coming into the city and I'll bring my stuff over, then we'll go meet Angie at the hospital."

"Slow down, Jim. What are you talking about?"

"Didn't she call you?"

"Who? Angie? No."

"I thought she called you!" he said angrily. "She didn't tell you?"

"Tell me what?"

"Darlene needs an operation. We're comin' in tomorrow."

"An operation? Darlene?" I knew I sounded like a parrot, but I was confused and disoriented. "What's wrong with her?"

"She has a brain tumor."

"What?"

"Yeah, so listen, I'll be in around two o'clock and I'll take you up to the hospital."

"Tomorrow?" I was reeling.

"Yeah. Angie's taking Jay over to Barbara's now. I'll tell her to call you when she gets back."

"Okay." I hung up, stunned, and sat down on the bed. How could this be? Darlene was one of the healthiest children I knew. How could she have a brain tumor? Jimmy was known for getting his facts mixed up. I told myself he was confused, and I'd wait to hear from Angie. Whatever was going on, it was probably far less dramatic than a brain tumor.

Two hours later Angie called, talking at even greater speed than Jimmy, falling into her usual habit of reciting the chores she had to do before they left for the hospital, throwing trivial details at me along with startling facts.

"Angie," I broke in as she was running down the arrangements she'd made for Jay's birthday on Monday. "Angie, how are *you*?"

"How am I? How do you think I am? Like you." I was silent, letting the weight and meaning of the words sink in. In those two little words she had conveyed a wealth of information.

The next day I learned the details: For weeks Darlene had been having headaches. Angie had taken her to the doctor, who prescribed medication and said if the headaches didn't go away they'd try migraine pills. Then she'd started to have dizzy spells, and once almost fell down the stairs. Soon she developed a mild limp. The doctor kept brushing off Angie's concerns, until she insisted that they do neurological testing. They'd discovered a grapefruit-sized tumor at the base of Darlene's brain.

In a daze, I phoned my friends and canceled my birthday party. I called my mother to tell her the news.

"Oh my God," she murmured sympathetically. But when I told her I was canceling my party, her sympathy quickly vanished. "Why do you have to do that?" Her tone was all too familiar to me; it was the tone that said I was overreacting.

"I don't *have* to," I told her. "I *want* to. I can't imagine having a party while this is going on, plus Jimmy will be staying here and it wouldn't be right."

"Don't be ridiculous!" She was incensed. "He'll just have to put up with it if he wants to stay at your place." She seemed to think I was being inconvenienced, taken advantage of.

Trying to explain to my mother why I could not party while my best friend's daughter was in the hospital for a brain tumor would be an exercise in futility. After all, she'd up and gone to Florida while Daryl was undergoing one operation, and had made herself scarce during the others. She'd spent her entire life avoiding pain and unpleasantness; she thought me demented for not doing the same.

I went to the play with my parents that night, barely able to remain in my seat for the two hours of inanity onstage ("Same Time Next Year" was pretty inane, especially given the mood I was in). I fidgeted during the show, and chain-smoked during intermission. My father asked in his typical clueless manner what was bothering me.

"Didn't Mommy tell you?"

"Tell me what?"

I sighed. My mother hadn't even considered Darlene's brain tumor significant enough to mention to him.

"Angie's daughter Darlene has a brain tumor."

"Oh?"

"Yeah."

"So what does it have to do with you?"

"For one thing," I said slowly, "she's my best friend. And for another, they'll be staying with me while she's in the hospital." To try and explain how this situation was arousing memories and emotions about Daryl's condition would be, I knew, fruitless—besides, these feelings were partly being aroused by my parents themselves.

My mother was insulted when I wanted to go right home rather than to Sardi's after the play. "My God," she said, shaking her head and looking at me as if I were a fool. "Don't you want to get your mind off it?"

"I can't."

"Of course you can! You don't want to," she huffed, as if I had committed some grave misdemeanor.

At the end of the evening I was relieved to get away from them—still, I felt absurdly guilty for spoiling *their* celebration of *my* birthday.

Jimmy arrived the next day in a manic state. We took a taxi to the hospital, him talking a mile a minute, me silent. When we got there I followed him through the hospital maze, up to pediatrics, into the waiting room, knowing the route by heart. While Jimmy went to get Angie, I stood looking out the window on a familiar scene. I couldn't help but remember all the time I'd spent at these windows, while Daryl lay in bed or on the operating table. One day he would probably be in that hospital bed again.

A terrifying thought struck me: *it could just as easily be Stacy.* After all, here was Darlene, seemingly healthy for a decade, about to go under the surgeon's knife. Was it possible that my constant concern about Daryl's health was unwarranted, that his life was in no greater danger than anyone else's? Worse, the thought of anything happening to Stacy, my healthy one, was a disaster beyond imagining.

A hand touched my arm and I turned to see Angie—or rather, Darlene's mother. Traces of mascara smudged her face, and though she was dressed, as always, in a perfectly coordinated outfit, her hair was askew and her face looked older. She literally threw herself into my arms and burst into sobs, muttering something I couldn't make out.

"What are you saying?"

"I'm sorry," she said, speaking distinctly into my ear. "I didn't know. I was just glad my kids were all right."

She had stepped into my shoes, had realized all I'd been through with Daryl, and how much she had not understood all these years. *I was just glad my kids were all right.*

I've tried to write the story of Darlene's illness in fictional form, but whenever I let someone else see it, they've said it's too melodramatic, that these things could not possibly have happened in real life, that the fictional story just didn't ring true. I don't know how to tell this story *without* it coming off as melodramatic—because this really is the way it happened. I may take poetic license here and there with dates and places, but I swear, this hospital scene and most of what follows is written almost exactly the way it happened.

Angie and I pulled ourselves together and wiped our tears. She told me that Darlene hadn't been told the severity of her condition, only that she needed an operation. We went inside to see her.

When I entered the room, the sensory assault that had begun when I walked into the hospital was further intensified. For a brief moment I saw not Darlene but Daryl in the bed. When I forced myself into reality, I realized I was in the role of visitor; I was my mother, my sister-in law—any one of the people who'd come to visit Daryl.

I kissed Darlene on the cheek. "What's a cute girl like you doin' in a place like this?"

"Don't ask me. I wanna go home. Where's Daryl and Stacy?"

"With their dad. Kids under twelve aren't allowed to visit."

"Couldn't Daryl use his connections?"

We all laughed, Darlene enjoying her own joke, her dimples deepening.

I sat in the chair, feeling awkward. This is what it had been like for visitors to come see Daryl. I'd hated them for their awkwardness, for prattling on about unrelated topics—or worse, their own operations. Then and there I swore that I would be an exemplary visitor: after all, if *I* didn't know how to do this, then nobody did. And yet...I realized that I really did not know how. If I talked about other things to distract Angie and Darlene, I'd be just as bad as anyone else. If I talked about Daryl's operations, I'd be doing what I most despised in others. I began to glimpse the dilemma faced by Daryl's visitors. I cast around in my head for a safe topic of conversation. "How's the food here?" I asked.

"Ugh. Gramma's bringing lasagna later."

I turned to Angie. "Your mother's coming?"

She rolled her eyes. "My mother, my father, my brothers, Kathy."

I loathed myself for the pinpricks of jealousy that struck me.

"Mommy," Darlene broke in, "how long am I gonna be here?"

"I told you, til they stop your headaches."

"But how are they gonna do that?" Darlene looked at me; I realized she had asked the question now, expecting that Angie would tell the truth in front of me. Her instincts were right.

"Darlene," Angie began, "I have to tell you something."

The child's face turned pale; somewhere inside she knew everything.

"You know the pictures they took of your head with the big round machine?"

Darlene nodded solemnly.

"The pictures showed some cells growing that shouldn't be there, and that's probably what's causing the headaches. They're going to take them out."

"With a knife?"

"Well, it's not exactly a knife. Anyway, they put you to sleep first and you don't feel a thing."

Darlene was silent a moment, taking this in. Then she said in a voice far older than her years, "I wanna call Daryl."

Angie looked at me; our eyes locked. It was all too much. I dialed the bedside phone and asked to speak to Daryl. His stepmother grudgingly went after him, putting me on hold for a full two minutes.

I handed the phone to Darlene. She said hello, then put her hand over the mouthpiece. "Could you please leave?" We were stunned, but did as she asked, and left her alone to talk to Daryl. It was hard to believe they were both ten years old.

Meanwhile, the waiting room was being taken over by Angie's family. Her mother, four foot eight, silver-haired, large bosom sagging beneath a faded housecoat, was yelling at everyone in her thick Italian accent, passing around lasagna on paper plates. Angie's father, a huge bear of a man who had always frightened me, stood with his back to the windows chewing on a cigar. Brothers, their wives, a few teenagers, all chattered away as if at a family reunion. I headed for the bathroom.

In the stall, I sobbed for a few minutes, not knowing for whom I was crying or what. I felt the way they say it feels to have acid flashbacks, reliving a frightening experience with the perspective of time. (It isn't always true that tragedy + time = comedy.) When I emerged from the stall, I found Barbara, Angie's sister-in-law, the woman who'd helped get me through Daryl's first year, combing her hair. We hadn't seen each other in nearly a decade.

"Barbara."

"Hi. How are you?"

"I'm okay. And you?"

"What do you think?" she said with a wry half smile.

I took out my makeup and began repairing my face. Barbara eyed me in the mirror. "I knew this would be harder on you than anyone."

"Why?"

"Because—it has to be bringing up memories."

Tears ruined my freshly applied mascara. "It is. But I keep thinking, if anyone should know how to behave here, it's me. If anyone can help Angie now...."

Barbara cut me off with a wave of her hand. "You won't be much help to her. You're going to be too fucked up."

"Oh God Barbara." I put the makeup away; it was useless. I took out my comb and tugged at a knot in my hair.

Barbara, who was a beautician and had done all of our hair when we were younger, gently took the comb from my hand and went to work on my mop. "You know," she said, manipulating my unruly hair with soothing expertise, "if anyone had told me the things that could happen, I never would have had kids." A few years ago Barbara had had a baby stillborn.

"Me too," I said grimly.

"You should go home."

"I can't."

"There are plenty of people here. You can come back tomorrow. You're gonna fall apart if you try to stay here all the time."

"You think?"

"Go home," she said, gently patting my hair into place one final time. "Everyone understands."

"They do?"

"Of course they do. I talked to Kathy last night, we both knew you'd be a wreck. Go on home. I'll tell Angie."

It stunned me that people knew how I'd react—that they had even thought about it beforehand—when I myself hadn't. Further, they'd never shown this much concern for me when I was actually going through Daryl's infancy, so I was puzzled that they were doing so now. Was it because we were older now, and understood the severity of the situation more than we had before? (I now know this is the case; in recent years we've all thoroughly analyzed and dissected the past.)

At home, I felt the same way I did whenever Daryl was in the hospital—disoriented, overwhelmed, unable to concentrate on anything. It didn't feel right to be away from the hospital. But it was late now; I decided to try and sleep, and return in the morning.

It's a good thing I went home; the next day was a marathon that would have tested the mettle of human beings far stronger than I.

It began in the morning, when the doctors conferred with Angie and Jimmy. They did not think they could get all of the tumor out, they said. Eventually the cells would proliferate again. Ultimately, they said, Darlene would probably die.

Most of the relatives had gone home, planning to return on Monday, the day of the operation. Angie, Jimmy, Kathy—who arrived midday—and I kept a vigil that lasted far into the following morning. From Darlene's room to cafeteria to waiting room we wandered together, or in pairs, talking, crying, ,smoking, sitting silently. Angie looked as if someone had thrown her up against a wall. For me, there was a surreal quality to the experience—not only the hospital and its memories, but being with Kathy and Angie again felt almost dreamlike. A few weeks later I wrote the following essay about that night.

The night they told us Darlene was going to die, Kathy, Angie and I sat around her bed while she slept. The lights were off; the hospital noise squeaked and clanged outside the room. We were sitting the way we were, Kathy and Angie on chairs, me on a footstool, slightly closer to Angie.

"Fifteen years later," Angie said, "and here we sit."

I wondered if Kathy minded that we were closer. She had always accepted her position gracefully, even seemed to enjoy it.

Kathy didn't need us as much as we needed each other. She knew exactly what she wanted, and began going steady with George a zillion years ago. We knew we only wanted what we were supposed to want. Today I am somewhat clearer about that. Angie is still carrying a lot of guilt about not really wanting it. I used to think, Angie is in the worst position. Now I know we are all in the same position.

The years faded away, and we reverted to our younger selves. Kathy and Angie were cleaning up the hospital room, good-naturedly criticizing each other's methods, while I followed them around talking non-stop. The giggles that came from our bellies, the adolescent girl giggles. Later came the mother's tears. Darlene said, Mommy, was a mother crying while I was asleep? She did not say a woman, she said, a mother.

Darlene's crisis is over. Angie's is not. It does no good for people to tell us our children will be okay, it doesn't mitigate the pain of seeing our babies handled by strangers, their scalps slit open and stitched together again. Nothing can wipe out the horrors we've seen.

They said she would die. I have never seen eyes like Angie's that night she thought her daughter was going to die. I cannot describe it. Who could.

Eight floors of this hospital are filled with terrified children. Does anyone know that the hospitals are full of our children? Do they know all the things that can happen to children? Besides the well publicized stuff like leukemia, cerebral palsy, muscular dystrophy? Does the world know about babies born with veins around their necks, strangling them? The rare blood diseases? The holes in the heart? Spinal lesions. Brain tumors. Missing limbs. Cataracts, yes, on babies. Hydrocephalus.

Talk to me, tell me my kid will be okay, tell me there's nothing to worry about. Until it's your kid. Then try to tell me.

For ten years everyone pretended that nothing was wrong with my son, and demanded that I pretend along with them. Everyone, that is, except his father, who pretends that nothing is right with him. Ten years of pretense have severely, maybe irreparably, damaged my son, our relationship, and me.

They made no pretense when they told Angie. They said, it is all over, you have birthed and raised her, and now it is over. The next day they removed every one of those nasty cells, and pronounced Darlene cured. They called it a miracle. Angie looked at me from across the room, acknowledging what only she and I knew: that her pain and fear were just beginning. When you are faced with a child's mortality, nothing is ever the same.

Patricia Neal had a son with hydrocephalus. The year she returned to the Academy awards show after recovering from a stroke, she got a standing ovation. I watched on TV and cried. She and her son made me feel less defective.

All the mothers with sick kids feel defective, like machines gone amok. One mother in the waiting room kept saying how thankful she was that her kids were all normal. Another mother said, if you say that word normal one more time, I will kill you.

I will no longer pretend that everything is okay, or that anything is normal. I will no longer try to ignore all the children in the hospitals of this great land. I will not shut up. I will not smile. I will not produce any more children.

But I will write. And I will speak out. Unlike Angie and Kathy, I am partially free. I alone have the time to sit at this typewriter. Their shadows fall over the page. I must do what they haven't the time or peace to do: I must tell our stories.

14

Do The Right Thing

I wish I had known then what I know now—a cliché full of truth. What I wish I had known was that mothers have enormous power; they need only to recognize and use it. I felt so much a victim for having motherhood forced on me that I could not see the role as a powerful one. Now I do: mothers who are confident of their ability to raise their children the way they see fit simply take control for granted. Had I exercised my maternal rights and the power inherent in birthing and loving my children, I never would have let Bob or anyone else interfere with my decisions or do my children any harm. New mothers should somehow be taught that maternal power is a birthright, because the way they mother their children will be strongly influenced by the way they perceive their role.

After the ordeal with Darlene and everything it put me through—not least of which was ruminating on the possibility of a child's death—I felt it imperative that I take my children back to live with me. Life was short, they were growing up under Bob's negative influence, and I was missing out on their childhood. I was still terrified of how Bob would react, that he might fight me for custody. When I finally got up the courage to tell him I wanted the kids back, though, he didn't miss a beat: "When?" he asked eagerly. I felt like a fool for my paranoid fantasies and all the time I'd wasted.

So I left the city, took my kids back to Woodstock, and resumed family life. The task of raising them single-handedly had become even more complicated; now I had to deal with the damage of a mother's abandonment and a father's abuse. They were not the same children I'd sent away; they were plagued with fear, insecurity, and anger.

I never managed to undo all the damage—in fact, I continued in my inept parenting to inflict more. But I began trying. I'm still trying.

I enrolled Daryl in a private school that was touted as "progressive," where he'd get more individualized attention. He loved the school—mostly, I suspect, because it made him feel special in a positive way for the first time in his life. More significantly, the student body was smaller and thus more socially manageable. His schoolmates tended to be from hippie type families like us, and were somewhat more tolerant of differences than were the kids in public school. Academically, though, the place was a disaster.

My first parent-teacher meeting was a shock; Daryl's five primary teachers sat as a unified bloc and bombarded me with the "facts": Daryl was lazy, Daryl was manipulative; Daryl's behavior showed that he received little home discipline; and why wasn't I helping him with his homework? I told them about his condition (which they'd already been informed of) and the seizure medication, and the perceptual problems we'd been told early on to expect; they brushed it all aside and insisted that he was lazy. As proof of this they pointed to Daryl's handwriting: large and shaky, it was the handwriting of a person taking daily doses of strong medication. They perceived it as indicating a lack of interest or focus due to poor study habits, for which I was partly to blame.

It was kindergarten all over again: Daryl still wouldn't, or as I was beginning to see, couldn't, color in the lines.

The school closed down the next year due to financial problems, and I enrolled Daryl in the only game in town—Onteora High School, in recent years acknowledged to be one of the worst public schools in New York State. Before the school year began I met with his guidance counselor and informed him of Daryl's condition—this was still a year or two before most schools developed an awareness of learning disabilities. I naturally expected the guidance counselor to brief all of Daryl's teachers.

But on my first parent-teacher night, Daryl's history teacher took me aside and said he was worried about Daryl—he often fell asleep in class, and he didn't seem to grasp the lessons. When I asked him if he knew that Daryl had a disability, his face reddened with anger. "No, I did *not* know!" he shouted. "Why didn't you tell me about this sooner?"

Other parents turned to stare at us; the teacher kept right on admonishing me. I was on the verge of tears; feebly I told him I'd assumed the guidance counselor had informed all of Daryl's educators. He proceeded to give me a stern teacherly lecture, the gist of which was that I was either an idiot or a negligent mother.

I arranged a meeting with all of Daryl's teachers. My intention was to educate the educators about my son's needs, but the meeting quickly turned into another session where I felt like Daryl and I were on trial. They had obviously discussed Daryl before I arrived; they seized control from the start, with an inquiry into Daryl's home environment.

They wanted to know exactly how I disciplined him. How did he get along with his sister? Did he miss his father? Did he mind coming from a "broken home?" They asked about our homework ritual, and informed me that I should be sitting at the table working on his assignments with him for at least two hours every evening.

In automatic self-protection mode, I turned inwardly to my political beliefs, a mixture of left-wing radicalism and anarchy, distrust of authority and rebellion against bureaucracy. I'd be damned if I would align myself with these unimaginative bozos; it was Daryl and me against the world—as it had always been.

In 1975 the Education of All Handicapped Children Act was passed, and educators fell all over themselves to address what they were suddenly mandated to regard as Daryl's right to special education. Quite honestly, I don't think that the folks at Onteora believed he had learning disabilities; it's just that governmental pressure was on them

to comply. Besides, many educators, in my observation, seem to actually revel in bureaucratic regulations.

In any case, in his junior and senior years of high school Daryl
received the first special education of his entire school career. This consisted of spending one period a day in a room with all kinds of disabled
people, ranging from those with dyslexia to the developmentally disabled, while a teacher trained in special ed helped him with his homework.

It was far too little far too late.

During these years I began researching alternative treatments for
everything that ailed Daryl: seizures, perceptual problems, emotional
problems. Vitamins, minerals and vegetables were the order of the day.
I investigated acupuncture and herbal treatment for hydrocephalus and
seizures—and learned they had nothing to offer. I had Daryl tested by
a psychological neurologist. For awhile he was put on a diet containing
no chemicals or sugar, which he, of course, refused to stick to.

In my quest for help I stumbled upon an agency that had something
tangible to offer: the Children's Rehabilitation Center in Kingston,
New York. A team of professionals there designed a program for Daryl
that included physical therapy, occupational therapy, psychological
counseling, and educational advocacy. Three times a week I drove him
to the center, and even got some counseling myself—though there was
a glitch: my request for a female counselor was interpreted as my having deep-seated problems with men, i.e., *my son*. Still, the center did
help Daryl somewhat; most important, he liked his counselors.

The problem, though, was that the other kids we encountered at the
center had much more severe, or at least more visible, disabilities than
Daryl. We'd sit in the waiting room alongside kids in wheelchairs, or
with limbs moving spasmodically. No teenage boy wants to identify
with severely disabled children, to see these kinds of people as his peer
group. Because of this, Daryl never felt one hundred percent okay
about the center. I asked his therapist if we could form some kind of

support group with others who were more like him, but it was an impossibility: as she pointed out, there weren't many "Daryl clones" living in the area.

This was always, and still remains, one of the unique and difficult issues of Daryl's life: he is not disabled enough to heartily join groups or activities designed for disabled people, but he is not "normal" enough to fully fit in with the non-disabled population. From my perspective, I'm still sitting in Kathy's kitchen wondering if I should leave him inside with the other babies.

In Daryl's senior year, while his classmates were filling out college applications and taking entry exams, Daryl spent six weeks being bused daily to a state vocational rehab center where he was tested in such skills as pipe-fitting and alphabetizing. The point, I was told, was to discover Daryl's aptitudes and enthusiasms; when the testing was over, they'd offer appropriate training and vocational assistance. I was excited by the prospects. Daryl's strongest interests were sports and music; he had several radios, including a short wave, and since he was a toddler he'd been creating tapes of funny news or music. My highest hope was that the vocational department would find a training program in the field of radio.

When the testing was over and it was time for Daryl's assessment conference, I brought along Mary, his counselor from the Children's Center. If there's just one pearl of wisdom I have to pass along to parents of kids with disabilities, it's this: *find an advocate for your child, preferably one with professional credentials, and always, but always, bring her or him along to educational or vocational meetings.*

A dozen "specialists" from the agency presented his test results and their analyses, and then offered their proposals—or rather, *proposal,* singular. Daryl, they said, should be placed in a "sheltered workshop" where people with disabilities "worked" at jobs such as stuffing lipstick into plastic packets, or lacing shoelaces into new sneakers; he would be paid something like seventeen cents an hour. This, they maintained, would engender self-confidence and prepare him for the work world. Proud of their proposal, they looked to me for my response.

I stared at them in abject horror. Daryl may not have excelled academically, but mentally he was sharp as a tack. Our friends, kids and adults alike, were highly entertained by his clever puns and witty jokes.. Everyone who knew Daryl—and in a small town like Woodstock, everyone did—considered him charming and amusing.

The State of New York saw no further than the results of uniform testing: their career path for Daryl was that he spend forty hours a week stuffing lipstick into plastic cases.

(I won't go off on a political tirade here, but a few months after this meeting I wrote an exposé for the local newspaper about the sheltered workshop system, whose purpose I am still convinced is to maintain a pool of cheap labor.)

Oh, and one more thing, the experts added: because of the possibility of having a seizure, Daryl would have to perform his duties from the safety of a well-cushioned chair.

"That'll sure give him confidence!" I blurted. It was the first comment I had made.

As one they looked solemnly at me, some shaking their heads sadly. They proceeded to tell me (and by the way, Daryl was right there listening) that my expectations for my son were unrealistic, that by denying him this "opportunity" I was condemning him to a lifetime of job failure.

Then Mary jumped into the fray. Calmly, without my emotional intensity —but without mincing words—she told Daryl's "team," exactly what she thought of their plan. She expounded on the potential she saw in Daryl—I noticed him sit up a bit straighter then—and that she felt the sheltered workshop program was inappropriate for him. She got the disapproving stares from the committee, but not the sad shakes of the head. In fact, they listened to Mary with far more respect than they did to me. The reason? Mary was a social worker, a professional, *one of them*. It is unfortunate but true that those who work with the disabled tend to treat mothers as obstacles. They operate on the premise that motherlove is irrational, that it blinds us to the realities of our child's situation, that we tend to see more potential in them than they actually have, and that we make unreasonable demands on schools and social service agencies.

(Note: Several years ago I obtained a Bachelor's degree through a university with an independent study program that gives college credit for life experience. For each area of learning I wrote up and documented my achievements. For the writing I had done, I received 33 credits. For public relations I received 12. For mothering a child with a disability I got three.)

I allowed Daryl to be in charge of his medication, so he would feel more responsible for his own health and less child-like and dependent on me. He walked to the drug store for his refills, kept his medicine in his own room, and took it according to the directions. I knew that he was angry about having to take daily medication, but I had no idea that he was acting on his anger—until he had a seizure and I discovered the empty pill bottle in his room.

This became a chronic problem: when I tried to monitor his drugs, he got furious at me; when I didn't, he stopped taking them. During the next three or four years Daryl had perhaps seven episodes of multiple seizures—and when a person passes from one convulsion to another without stopping (status epillepticus), it can be life threatening. Each time he was rushed to the hospital by ambulance. Each time his neurologist gave him a lecture. Each time I tried reasoning with him. And each time he promised it wouldn't happen again.

Daryl was using whatever was at his disposal in the service of teenage rebellion. I began to joke that, while most parents worry about their kids *taking* drugs, I worried about mine *not* taking them. But it was no joking matter. Once he stopped breathing –luckily we were in the emergency room when it happened.

I became so accustomed to the whole process that upon arrival in the ER I would instruct the doctor exactly what to do and give him the neurologist's home number. On one such occasion the doctor on call, who spoke very little English, left Daryl convulsing while he perused a medical text to find out what amount of medication to give him. I kept telling him I knew the amount, but he ignored me, and finally became insulted by my pleas to call Daryl's regular doctor. A friend was with me, a woman who happened to be a nurse; she got into a shouting match with him, saying, among other things, "As a medical professional I'm ashamed of you."

To make Daryl take his medicines I tried everything, including "tough love." Whereas I'd always stayed with Daryl in the emergency room until his release, after one episode I left him in the hospital bed, saying, "You're on your own, kiddo," and did not return until the next day to drive him home.

Only in his twenties did Daryl stop messing around with his medication, and it took a dramatic event for him to do so. His doctor asked him if he'd been trying to kill himself by not taking his medication, and Daryl casually replied that yes, he had. To this day I don't know if this was true or not—I don't think Daryl even knows—but the result was that the doctor, acting according to state law, sent him directly to the psychiatric ward. It took me and an ACLU lawyer two weeks to get him released. He never skipped his medication again.

Or maybe the reason he changed was far less dramatic. Shortly after the psyche ward episode, Daryl moved to California and we went to see a new neurologist. Now, the one he'd had in upstate New York was the only, I repeat, *the only*, neurologist for fifty miles. In Oakland California the choices were far greater—and, it turned out, so was the quality of treatment. On Daryl's first visit the doctor talked—or rather listened—to Daryl for a good half-hour. He asked, among other things, why Daryl skipped his medication. Daryl told him how the pills made him sleepy and lethargic. The doctor ordered a slew of tests, then began reducing Daryl's dosage until he reached the lowest level possible that still prevented seizures. Daryl is still sometimes tired, but not anywhere near as much as he used to be. More important, he trusts and respects his doctor, who was willing to take his concerns seriously and let him play a bigger part in his own treatment.

In describing a few select incidents about Daryl's education, vocational planning and medical history I've been attempting to portray, as briefly as possible, the kind of life we led. These days a slew of badly needed books is emerging that are resources for parents of children with disabilities. But I have yet to see a book that tells it like it is from a parent's point of view. The events I've described are the tip of the iceberg, representing many events in our lives—these were not the only ones, or even the worst that occurred.

When I began writing this memoir, I thought that Daryl's infancy was the most difficult aspect of raising him. In hindsight, I see that the teenage years were just as difficult.

Further, it isn't over. We've all heard the cliché that parenting continues for the rest of our lives; when the child has a disability, this truth is intensified many times over. Daryl's issues did not magically end when he reached adulthood; they continue to this day. To briefly summarize a few more: he spent a year in a special education program at a college, which was about as effective as the one he attended in his senior year of high school. He took classes at a community college, continuing to struggle academically until I convinced him that perhaps college was not his cup of tea. He's worked as a day care provider, a copy machine operator, and in an antique furniture store. In all of his jobs he's had problems, including one in which a job coach from the state of California assisted him. He's done volunteer work at a food program and a first aid organization. He attended massage school where the instructors weren't flexible enough to provide him with the kind of learning tools he needed, and whom I came close to suing.

At 36 he's given up on looking for jobs; he lives on SSI benefits and says he has no desire to work. It's become, finally, too much for him—the struggle, the explanations to employers, the failures.

For years I was on his case to find a job, always coming up with new ideas and resources for him. About a year ago I decided to cease and desist. I've come to accept that his life is what it is. For someone who's been through what Daryl has been through, he's actually doing quite well: how many bachelors, after all, cook themselves healthy meals nightly, do their laundry once a week and keep their apartments reasonably clean?

The only thing I can do anymore for Daryl is to accept him as he is, and be a good friend to him. By doing this, our relationship has improved dramatically, and I no longer view him as a burden but as an asset in my life. Finally, I'm deriving more pleasure than pain out of being a parent.

15

Just The Way You Are

August 3, 1995

A photograph. Daryl stands in the center of a crowd of people toasting him with champagne. He is laughing with unselfconscious joy, perhaps sharing a joke with Stacy, who stands, also laughing, next to him. In the background is a middle-aged woman holding a serving platter. It is Daryl's thirtieth birthday.

Most of the guests at Daryl's party were my friends; he has very few of his own in California. But though he met these people through me, he's formed independent relationships with them. Maybe it's because he was around so many strangers during his childhood, or maybe because he felt an unbridgeable gap between himself and people his own age—but throughout his life he's formed close personal bonds with older people. At the party was Phyllis, my photographer friend, whom he often assists on photo shoots; Joss, with whom he watches the Superbowl; Andrew, who goes to ball games with him; Laurie, who cuts his hair; Sandra, who served for a time on the Board of Directors of the Hydrocephalus Association.

Someone put on a tape that Daryl and I had recorded down on Fisherman's Wharf, singing Billy Joel's "Just The Way You Are." Mortified when my off-key singing came screeching out of the speakers, I ran into the bathroom to hide. Laurie followed and tried to persuade me to come out.

"Do you know how many mothers would be *ecstatic* to have made a recording like this with one of their children?" she asked. Humbled, I came back out to hear everyone applauding and laughing as the last off-kilter notes rang out.

One person wasn't laughing: Darlene's eyes were brimming with tears.

Now thirty-six, Daryl lives independently, in his own apartment, four miles from me. His sister, now thirty-four, lives in Los Angeles with her husband and two fabulous little boys. She and I are still working through issues that arose from having disability in the family. In *Special Kids Need Special Parents*, Judith Loseff Lavin maintains that siblings of children with disabilities often grow up to be more compassionate and tolerant adults. In our case that is certainly true: Stacy involves herself in Daryl's life and cares a great deal about him. She's a therapist who facilitates support groups for mothers of newborns. Someday, she told me, she wants to specialize in treating mothers of children with disabilities.

Nonetheless, our relationship has been fraught with miscommunication, misunderstandings, frustration and deep pain. Aside from the everyday garden-variety challenges of the mother-daughter relationship, we've had to contend with the extra issues that arise from having a disability in the family. Throughout her childhood Stacy suffered neglect: I had rather limited attention for mothering to begin with, and the lion's share of what I did have went to the child with the greatest need. . She was such an independent, seemingly healthy child, psychologically as well as physically, that I simply took it for granted that she'd be all right. We've had many crying conversations; I've apologized to her repeatedly, and she says she's forgiven me—but the repercussions from the past continue to plague the way we relate to one another now.

Being a grandmother has been, for me, the ultimate reward of motherhood. Many mothers feel this way, but as with so much else in our family, the feelings—at least my feelings—are even more intense. Stacy's sons adore Daryl, or "Uncle Dayel," who reads them stories, chases them around the yard and snaps photos of them at every opportunity.

Otherwise, Daryl's social life is almost non-existent. His last shunt revision was performed when he was twenty-four. It's been over five years since he had a seizure episode; the last was in the car in the middle of the night, and I flagged down a passing motorist for help. After that I bought a cell phone.

We talk on the phone every day: if Daryl doesn't answer for any length of time I imagine he's having a seizure in the shower; several times I've driven to his place and let myself in with my key. He complains about this kind of maternal smothering, and I can't blame him—but neither can I stop worrying. I'm still confused about how much to watch over him and how much to let him live a "normal" life.

But I've learned to accept Daryl, water on the brain and all. It took a long time to learn how to be his mother, and though I still suffer for his pain and difficulties, I no longer deny his condition, pity myself because of it, or expect him to be something other than who he is.

One thing that I continue to do is wonder what "caused" Daryl's hydrocephalus. In recent years studies have proven definitively that a lack of folic acid before and during pregnancy is a primary cause of disorders of the central nervous system in newborns. Doctors now instruct pregnant women, and all women of childbearing age, to take supplemental pills. Nutritionally, folic acid is found in green leafy vegetables. I have no problem believing that Daryl's hydrocephalus resulted from my poor nutritional habits: throughout my adolescence I lived primarily on chocolate chip cookies and Coca cola, and my eating habits didn't improve when I got pregnant. When you think about it, the fact that I, a middle-class American girl, suffered from malnutrition substantial enough to cause a birth defect in my child is simply outrageous. We as a society have got to stop reproducing children in utter ignorance.

Whatever acceptance I've managed to reach didn't come easy, nor did it come soon enough. By the time I adjusted to what I'd been landed with, Daryl was an adult. I've spent the past decade trying to compensate for the damage I did in his early years. I still see the results of that damage all the time. For instance, although Daryl is an avid sports fan, he doesn't participate in any sports activities himself; he hardly even exercises. I've heard him talking to his best friend about this, acknowledging that in his childhood everyone hovered so much over him, afraid he'd break his shunt or get hurt in some other way, that it made him fearful of physical activity. Well, I was the one who hovered over him so fearfully, only half-heartedly trying to teach him to ride a bicycle (he never did learn how). In my defense, it wasn't only me: his neurologist, for instance, insisted that he shouldn't be allowed to go swimming; the doctor had once been sued by a child who died having a seizure in a swimming pool. I defiantly let him swim—and worried every second he was in the water.

Still, I did enough hovering to feel guilty about it now, when Daryl watches basketball games wishing he was playing. I regularly apologize to him for not having encouraged him to overcome his limitations. He takes my guilt in stride, joking

that he was sent into this world to "test" me, that he is periodically assessing my progress. I joke back that I don't want to completely pass the test, because if I ever stop learning it will be because he's gone. For most of his life I've been terrified that I might outlive him—but the older I get the less I worry about this.

The majority of parents of children with disabilities do, in fact, worry a great deal about death—but it's the reverse scenario that haunts them. They fear that if they die first, there'll be no one to take care of their children. Again, here I stand, with a very different—and much less selfless—fear. I've thought recently about the possibility that Daryl might deteriorate as he ages, necessitating greater care than he needs now. I don't want to be a seventy-year-old caretaker. I don't want to have to help a fifty-year-old man go to the bathroom and brush his teeth. The very thought of it makes me long for an early death.

One thing that's helped me with my guilt is finding other people in my situation. When I moved to San Francisco (Daryl moved out here shortly afterwards) I discovered the Hydrocephalus Association. Years ago I'd met the founders of The Guardians of Hydrocephalus in New York, but most of their members lived in one geographical area, and their primary purpose was raising funds for research. The Association has a broader national base and a wider array of services: education, advocacy, and support. When I attended my first parents' meeting, and told the others my age and Daryl's, they literally gasped.

"You're a pioneer," someone said admiringly.

Although a few of the members' children were then teenagers, most of them had infants, toddlers and school-age kids.

It was a revelatory moment: Though I was vaguely aware that Daryl had been one of the earliest children to be shunted, the ramifications of that hit me for the first time. Daryl is among the first generation of infants born with hydrocephalus to reach adulthood—and it's a fairly small group of people. I'd been swimming in completely uncharted waters all his life. The anger I'd felt about the lack of information and resources was natural, but hardly justified: how could there be information and resources about people who did not exist? Now I know why, when Daryl was a baby, none of the doctors would tell us how long people with hydrocephalus live: *they had no idea.* At the time of Daryl's birth, the shunt operation was fairly new, and there were few survivors.

Consequently, we are only beginning to discover what issues children with this condition face as they mature. (We've also discovered that many elderly people develop the condition, misdiagnosed until recently.)

I became active in the Association, first attending conferences and later, when I was on the Board of Directors, helping to organize them.

I'm no longer as involved with the group's operation, but I regularly write articles and reviews for the quarterly newsletter.

Moving west also brought me to Berkeley, the center of the Disability Rights Movement. I began to write articles about disability for both mainstream publications and those aimed directly at the disabled population. I interviewed and befriended people with disabilities both common and rare. I learned, and continue to learn, an enormous amount from this community. Knowing them has put my own life and struggle, as well as Daryl's, into perspective, and has made me as militant about the rights of the disabled as I've always been about all oppressed groups. I'm still angry—but now I know my anger is justified, and I can act upon it constructively. My work around disability has increased my self-esteem and decreased my sense of isolation. It's done the same for Daryl, who frequently accompanies me to disability events and reads the same books on disability as I do, as well as my writing on the topic.

At the last hydrocephalus conference we attended, Daryl had his picture taken with about forty other people like himself. Though most are considerably younger, a handful of them are his age, and he's befriended one or two with whom he regularly communicates by phone and email.

These days when a child is born with hydrocephalus—or any chronic condition—social services step in with information and support, even financial assistance. Attitudes toward people with disabilities are changing—slowly, but dramatically. Services have proliferated, the general public isn't as ignorant as they used to be, and people with disabilities are much more visible—they're not hidden away in the attic or even the living room, as they were once upon a time. Our society has grown much more tolerant towards deviations from the "norm." In fact, things have changed so much that I suspect some people won't believe some of the things I've described in this book (hell, they didn't believe me back then).

Not that the able-bodied (ABs as they're called by those in the know) population is entirely enlightened: I still hear stories from parents about insensitive doctors, uncooperative schools, teasing classmates. Sadly, most adults with disabilities have limited social lives and are isolated and lonely. Another thing that disturbs me is the wide acceptance of—and even social pressure to—abort a fetus found in utero to be "deformed." I am by no stretch of the imagination opposed to abortion—I have actively worked to ensure that it remain legal. However, even people who oppose abortion tend to relax their "morals" when it comes to birth "defects." I've heard conversations in which it's taken for granted that if a fetus is found to be "defective" the mother will abort; furthermore, if she chooses to have the child, she is often judged for it. This signifies a widely accepted attitude that people with disabilities simply should not be allowed to live—or at least should not be brought into the world.

As a proponent of abortion rights and the mother of a child with a disability, I've had to look hard at this issue. Suppose I had known about Daryl's condition while he was in my womb, and suppose abortion was legal (it wasn't) at the time? To be honest, I am pretty sure I would have opted to terminate the pregnancy.

And then I wouldn't have Daryl. I would have been deprived of my best friend, the one person on this planet who loves me unconditionally. Not be allowed to live? Not be brought into the world? Huh?

16

New York Mets vs. Yankees
2000

A subway series: Daryl and I were ecstatic. Though we no longer lived in the Big Apple, we hadn't quite dragged our hearts out to San Francisco. Every transplanted New Yorker remains fiercely loyal to something about the homeland, whether it's the bagels, the pizza or baseball. Born in the home of the Bronx Bombers, I'm a diehard Yankee fan; Daryl is devoted to the Mets, the team that was born just a few years before him. We bet on our respective teams: if his won, I'd buy him a Mets jacket; if mine won, I'd get a Yankee cap.

Of course, the Yankees won. Daryl watched miserably as the Mets, in their inimitable way, made a series of blunders, and I cackled with glee, calling them the keystone cops of baseball. When it was over, he was miserable and I was ecstatic.

"Why do you insist on being a Met fan?" I asked him for the hundredth time. "It only makes you miserable."

"I know, Ma, I've suffered so much with these guys."

"It's a choice," I told him. "If you wanna be happy, all you have to do is become a Yankee fan."

Happiness is not always so simple: but, in the area of baseball at least, I've learned that sometimes you can make a choice. Daryl, unfortunately, has yet to learn this.

But I bought him the Mets jacket anyway.

0-595-21544-0